AF541052

GOOD GOVERNANCE

GOOD GOVERNANCE
Initiatives in India

Editors

E. VAYUNANDAN
Reader, Public Administration
Indira Gandhi National Open University
New Delhi

DOLLY MATHEW
Reader, Public Administration
Indira Gandhi National Open University
New Delhi

Prentice-Hall of India Private Limited
New Delhi-110 001
2003

Rs. 395.00

GOOD GOVERNANCE: Initiatives in India
Edited by E. Vayunandan and Dolly Mathew

ISBN-81-203-2203-7

Published by Asoke K. Ghosh, Prentice-Hall of India Private Limited, M-97, Connaught Circus, New Delhi-110001 and Printed by Syndicate Binders, B-167, Okhla Industrial Area, Phase I, New Delhi-110020.

Contents

Preface .... *vii*

Contributors .... *ix*

1. Introduction 1
   ◆ *E. Vayunandan* and *Dolly Mathew*

2. Development and Reforms in Good Governance with Special Reference to India 16
   ◆ *E. Vayunandan*

3. Governance for Development: Issues and Strategies 28
   ◆ *D.K. Ghosh*

4. Bureaucracy: Changing Roles and Relationships A Transformative Agenda 39
   ◆ *Dolly Mathew*

5. Responsive Administration of the Criminal Justice System in India 46
   ◆ *K.K. Sharma*

6. E-governance: Options and Opportunities 52
   ◆ *P.K. Mehrotra* and *Alok Ranjan*

7. Achieving Excellence Through E-governance 62
   ◆ *J.C. Kapoor*

8. Information Technology and Governance 70
   ◆ *Sanjay Jaju*

9. E-governance by Information Technology: Initiatives of a Metropolitan City 86
   ◆ *Vijay Rattan*

10. Issues and Strategies in Good Governance with Special Reference to Karnataka 95
   ◆ *Vivek Kulkarni*

11. FRIENDS: An E-governance Project of Kerala **102**
◆ *Aruna Sunderarajan*

12. Governance for Development: New Initiative Gramsat Pilot Project, Orissa **108**
◆ *S.P. Nanda*

13. E-Governance for Improved Service: Choices Made by Tamil Nadu **121**
◆ *M. Anandakrishnan*

14. Perspectives on Democratic Decentralized Governance for Rural Development in Mizoram **127**
◆ *R.N. Prasad* and *Lalneihzovi*

15. Lessons in Organising Self Help: A Case Study of the Sukhomajri Water Resources Management Project **136**
◆ *Ramanjit Kaur Johal*

Index ***143***

Preface

The focus of public administration today is on good governance. We, as faculty of public administration in the Indira Gandhi National Open University, organised a conference in August 2001 at New Delhi, focusing on the issues and strategies of good governance. The issues and strategies raised and brought forth by learned speakers from various backgrounds have motivated us to bring out this edited volume—*Good Governance: Initiatives in India*.

This book focuses on how to make the public service delivery system in India, efficient and effective. The underlying theme of this book, therefore, is public service delivery. It addresses to the issues of good governance in two different perspectives: one pertaining to the efficient delivery of public services and second, to the strategies that render it effective. The first deals with the problem areas while the second refers to the various methods and techniques to address these problem areas. The governance of public service delivery involves vital issues of accountability, transparency, equity, efficiency, effectiveness, participation, responsiveness, decentralisation, and ethics. The strategies that cater to these issues are threefold: the first, based on reforming the administration that includes administration restructuring, reinvention, realignment, re-engineering, and rethinking; the second, based on the application of Information and Communication Technology and e-governance; and the third, based on decentralisation that includes democratic decentralisation through people's participation, interactive policy making, and privatisation. The book primarily emphasizes on these strategies that relate to

- Increasing the efficiency and effectiveness of the government and administration.
- Enhancing the role of Information and Communication Technology and e-governance.
- Accomplishing the decentralisation of governance.

This book will help the readers to comprehend the evolution and development of good governance in the national and international spheres; changing roles and relationships of bureaucracy in respect of the governance reforms; initiatives in ICT and e-governance at various levels—centre, state, and local; and democratic decentralisation and self-help initiatives. It will also serve as a beneficial reference for students and persons from varied and diversified fields, such as management, social sciences, computers and information sciences, electronic media, and education.

Our efforts in bringing out this book could never have materialised without the constant guidance and support of our faculty members. We profusely thank our faculty members Prof. Pardeep Sahni, Dr. Alka Dhameja, Dr. Uma Medury, and Dr. Durgesh Nandini. Ms. Geeta deserves special mention for her commendable work in offering her secretarial skills. Mr. Pratap Nagaraj and Mr. Rajeev Sharma are also worthy of our thanks for their time to time skilled help.

Our family members have held us as the backbone during the completion of this entire work. Our special thanks go to them.

E. VAYUNANDAN
DOLLY MATHEW

Contributors

The book contains papers contributed by the following:

1. **Dr. E. VAYUNANDAN**
   Reader
   Faculty of Public Administration
   Indira Gandhi National Open University
   New Delhi

2. **Dr. DOLLY MATHEW**
   Reader
   Faculty of Public Administration
   Indira Gandhi National Open University
   New Delhi

3. **Mr. D.K. GHOSH**
   Registrar
   Indian Institute of Technology
   Mumbai

4. **Dr. K.K. SHARMA**
   Reader, Public Administration
   Department of Evening Studies
   Panjab University
   Chandigarh

5. **Mr. P.K. MEHROTRA**
   Chief Secretary
   Government of Madhya Pradesh

6. **Prof. ALOK RANJAN**
   Madhya Pradesh Academy of Administration
   Bhopal, Madhya Pradesh

7. **Prof. J.C. KAPOOR**
   IIPA, New Delhi

8. **Mr. SANJAY JAJU**
Commissioner
Visakhapatnam Municipal Corporation
Visakhapatnam

9. **Prof. VIJAY RATTAN**
Department of Public Administration
Directorate of Correspondence Studies
Panjab University, Chandigarh

10. **Mr. VIVEK KULKARNI**
Secretary, IT
Government of Karnataka
Bangalore, Karnataka

11. **Ms. ARUNA SUNDERARAJAN**
Secretary, IT
Government of Kerala

12. **Mr. S.P. NANDA**
Secretary
Government of Orissa

13. **Mr. M. ANANDAKRISHNAN**
Former Advisor, IT
Government of Tamil Nadu

14. **Prof. R.N. PRASAD**
Department of Public Administration
Mizoram University
Aizwal, Mizoram

15. **Mr. LALNEIHZOVI**
Visiting Fellow and Research Scholar
Department of Public Administration
Mizoram University
Aizwal, Mizoram

16. **Dr. RAMANJIT KAUR JOHAL**
Lecturer
Department of Public Administration
Panjab University
Chandigarh

Note: The authors were holding the above mentioned positions/ designations at the time of the papers were written.

Introduction

— E. Vayunandan
— Dolly Mathew

This book focuses on good governance and highlights various initiatives undertaken in India for effective public service delivery. The government should not only be able to afford, but should also be willing to formulate new strategies for effective public service delivery. Such strategies include developing partnerships, mobilising civil society groups, re-positioning bureaucracy, decentralisation and the use of information and communication technology (ICT). The book takes up the issues and strategies of public service delivery in India and focuses on the new role of the government and the bureaucracy. It also demonstrates the use of ICT in information sharing, communication and transactions, and decentralised governance—all potent tools of efficient public service delivery.

PUBLIC SERVICE DELIVERY

Various agencies are involved in delivering public services. These include the government, the private sector and the civil society groups. It is essential that the services should be responsive to users needs. In the context of good governance, Willy McCourt points out that service delivery should focus on three important points:

1. Ensuring performance. Today public service agencies have to adhere to service standards. They have to meet the objectives rather than just follow the rules. They are required to develop standards to monitor and evaluate service quality and also provide for public reporting of the results. Most countries today have citizen's charters, which make these agencies accountable to their citizens. These charters lay down the quality of services that these agencies are expected to provide.

2. Developing competition. Contracts are awarded through market testing.

These contracts are performance indicators. With competition and internal and external bidding, performance gets enhanced at three stages: in bidding for the contract, in monitoring compliance and in re-bidding at the end of the contract period. This results in services becoming result-driven, transparent, accountable and responsive to customers, as feedback really matters.

3. Responsive service. Public service agencies have to lay down service standards and use customer surveys to get information on service users' preferences and views. The emphasis on total quality management improves the quality of products and services by gearing up the total operations of an organisation to achieve a quantified standard of quality. Quality assurance is given importance.

Thus, public service delivery in good governance is ensured by the following:

1. Establishing service standards.
2. Evaluating performance on the basis of output and quality.
3. Improving public perception by making the services citizen-friendly.
4. Utilising ICT, consumer care training and grievance redressal to bring the public service agencies closer to people.
5. Delivering the services in an efficient, effective and timely manner with concern and courtesy.
6. Giving importance to the legal rights and entitlements of citizens.
7. Engaging in efforts to enable consultation and participation of people in decision-making. Consultative mechanisms such as consumer surveys and public hearings provide inputs from people.
8. Improving people's accessibility to services by bringing the delivery points closer to them.

For an effective public service delivery, governance has to be responsive, responsible, accessible, accountable, result-oriented, transparent, efficient, effective and collaborative. Today, not only have users of public services become enlightened about the quantity and quality of services, but they are also involved in the process of service delivery through various civil society groups. The re-engineering of government machinery, use of ICT and decentralised governance have made this possible. We will be discussing the role of administration, ICT, e-governance and decentralised governance as these are the vital strategies for addressing the issues of governance in service delivery.

ADMINISTRATION AND SERVICE DELIVERY

Reforms in governance focus on the efficient delivery of public services. The entire government machinery and the bureaucracy have to be citizen-oriented. They need to know the services they render, the beneficiaries they have to cater to and satisfy. This calls for re-engineering of the administrative system. The Action Plan for Effective and Responsive Government formulated at the Conference of Chief Ministers of the States in May, 1997, has laid down the following three measures to re-engineer the entire administration.

- Making administration accountable and citizen-friendly.
- Ensuring transparency and right to information.
- Taking steps to cleanse and motivate the civil services.

Making Administration Accountable and Citizen-friendly

Service delivery becomes efficient by making the administration accountable and citizen-friendly. The latter has to be sensitive to people's needs. The focus should be on the formulation and implementation of citizen's charters, redressal of public grievances, decentralisation and devolution of powers and review of laws, regulations and procedures, so as to make administration accountable and citizen-friendly.

Various steps have been taken in this regard. The Department of Administrative Reforms and Public Grievances in the Ministry of Personnel, Public Grievances and Pensions, is coordinating the formulation and implementation of citizen's charters. Sixty-eight central government organisations have so far issued such, charters. About 20 states have also issued more than 180 citizen's charters. The Department of Administrative Reforms and Public Grievances has conducted evaluation studies of certain charters (Tandon et al).

Likewise, senior officers have been appointed as directors of grievances in every ministry. Time limits have been laid down for the disposal of grievances. Further, software for networked monitoring of the public grievance redressal mechanism has also been developed. A web-enabled version of this software is being installed in all ministries to provide instant access to citizens. The Commission on the Review of Administrative Laws, set up in 1998, has reviewed 2500 laws, suggested repeal of 1400 laws and amendments to 2140 laws. Five committees on procedural reforms have been constituted to address the issues of procedural delays in financial approvals, recruitment in general, and appointments to senior positions in particular, vigilance matters and service litigation (Tandon et al).

Ensuring Transparency and Right to Information

There is a need to introduce greater transparency in the functioning of government and public bodies, and ensure widespread and easy access to all information, except that excluded by law, relating to government operations, decisions and performance. The Freedom of Information Bill placed before the Parliament in July 2000, seeks to amend the Official

Secrets Act. In states like Rajasthan, the right to information bill has been passed and people's organisations like *Mazdoor Kisan Shakti Sangathan* and *Jan Sunwai* have enabled villagers to demand information about the details of expenditure on development works in their villages. Likewise, different ministries have set up information and facilitation counters. Computerised access to information from public offices has also been made available. The Department of Post and Telecommunications and the Life Insurance Corporation have set up customer care centres to provide information and redressal of grievances across the counter. There are proposals to set up computerised web-based multi-utility centres of central and state governments to provide information and a wide variety of services to the citizens, pertaining to the payment of bills, filing of returns, registration of vehicles, downloading applications for passport, reservations, submission of applications, rules and regulations, etc.

Taking Steps to Cleanse and Motivate the Civil Services

It is necessary to enhance the obligation of the civil servants to the government and the Constitution of India, to make them accessible and responsive to the people in terms of quality of services, timeliness and courtesy, and increase their readiness to encourage participation and partnerships with citizens groups for responsive government. Developing policy analysis skills, human resources development, rewarding achievement, instilling public service accountability, redundancy management, improving quality of services, introduction of quality management approach, incorporating ICT, improving skills pertaining to the management of finance, public reporting and emphasis on ethics and values are some of the strategies that can lead to administrative reforms and will have a positive impact on citizens' perceptions.

Various efforts have been made to motivate and cleanse the civil services. A code of ethics has been formulated and is being considered by the Government of India. The code provides safeguards against release of sensitive information and abuse of official position, and provides for continuous improvement of the civil services through professionalism and teamwork. It is now proposed to make the Central Vigilance Commission a statutory body, which puts a check on the corrupt practices of officials. Likewise, the Lokpal Bill has been approved by the cabinet for introduction to the Parliament. Various states have also set up Lokayuktas. This will effectively deal with corruption cases. Similarly, constitution of a high-powered Civil Services Board, or extending the jurisdiction of the existing Public Service Commissions may guard against politicisation of postings, transfers and promotion (Minocha).

The Ministry of Personnel, Public Grievances, and Pensions is implementing a project, initially in training institutes, to introduce total quality management in the government. Likewise, a new scheme to undertake pilot projects in administrative reforms has been sanctioned with effect from 2000–2001. There are proposals to implement projects in the fields of evaluation, benchmarking, application of ICT in government, research studies in administrative reforms, development of knowledge management systems and assessment of quality in government (Tandon et al.).

ICT AND E-GOVERNANCE IN SERVICE DELIVERY

ICT has touched all facets of the life of a common man. Richard Heeks and David Mundy have defined IT as computing and telecommunications technologies that provide automatic means of handling information. Victor JJM Bekkers writes that IT was primarily a technology that was used for calculation purposes. During the last ten years we have seen that IT has encompassed information as well as communication technology. The development of network technologies, the coupling of databases, telematics, groupware and all kinds of search systems have stressed the importance of other uses, besides calculation.

ICT has the potential for communication. Time, place and physical presence are no longer essential. It offers new possibilities for establishing all kinds of links between people and organisations. Their interactions become wired and the quality and quantity of interaction increases. It enhances the transparency and access to organisations. Information systems of libraries, government agencies can be consulted through the Internet, while intranets make it possible to share information throughout the organisation. The functioning of different organisations and government departments can also be integrated. The boundaries of an organisation become electronically permeable. With computers it is possible to analyse data, trends and development in policies, and know the outcomes. There is more transparency and this leads to monitoring and surveillance. Network technology has made virtual reality possible, wherein a person can work and shop sitting at home. Moreover, in all information processing systems, communication and interaction are facilitated.

The application of ICT has been found to be highly useful in governance, which is known as e-governance, or electronic governance. E-governance plays the following important roles:

1. Increases efficiency by automation, computerisation and networking.
2. Supports effective decentralised decision-making by providing an efficient information flow.
3. Increases accountability of the public service agencies to citizens.
4. Improves resource management.
5. Offers the various departments and agencies involved in public service provision the facility of effective communication between each other and effective interface with the citizens.
6. Increases the accessibility of individual citizens to information and services and allows them to influence government operations.

7. Provides comprehensive database which helps policy makers to design, formulate and evaluate policies.
8. Facilitates the strategic planning process which helps organisations to clearly lay down the objectives, goals, programmes and projects.
9. Enables reduction of paperwork with the use of e-mail and electronic data interchange.
10. Enables marketisation by supplying information related to the market and enhances public service.

The advantages of e-governance can be derived by:

(a) Proper planning and management for digital governance.
(b) Application of computerised text processing, information storage and retrieval and communication systems.
(c) Providing accessibility.
(d) Adopting new technologies.
(e) Bringing in qualified and trained personnel.
(f) Continuous assessment of the ramifications of ICT.

E-governance facilitates service delivery by providing integrated services through a single window system, by combining allied services in a single office, reducing the levels of interaction between the citizen and the administration, increasing the citizens' choices in how services have to be delivered, providing accessibility to people, irrespective of time and place, and assuring the quality of services. It helps in improving the provision of public services by enabling increased coordination between various departments. Thus, there is smooth flow of information between various agencies and this fosters quick services. Databases related to public services enable the setting up of Management Information System (MIS) which helps decision makers to plan for public services. Also, monitoring becomes easy. This helps in giving the necessary feedback to improve upon services. Extra costs can also be avoided.

Undoubtedly, the application of ICT requires vast infrastructure and the expertise of professionals. One needs to make an assessment of the benefits and costs involved in ICT ventures. It may be useful to initially go for computerised, front-end interface for the people to access services, without waiting for back-end computerisation, as has been done in the case of the FRIENDS Project in Kerala. The attitudes and motivation of the personnel and people are to be groomed through training. E-governance should focus on indigenous needs, the socio-cultural environment and on the poor and the marginalised. Involvement of self-help groups to undertake supplemental services in e-governance initiatives should be promoted as this can help in acceptance of technology by the people.

The Ministry of Personnel, Public Grievances and Pensions has been entrusted with the task of setting up a National Institute of Smart Government. The institute would attempt to raise societal awareness and capability in SMART (simple, moral, accountable, responsive and transparent) governance by promoting policies and practices which reinforce a hassle free environment for citizens. It would be the focal referral site for any information on solutions, benchmarks and best practices within the country and abroad (Tandon et al).

ICT has made services amenable to people living in cities and villages. The Gyandoot programme in Madhya Pradesh, the e-seva network in Andhra Pradesh, FRIENDS in Kerala, the Saukaryam Project in Visakhapatnam, the Gramsat Project in Orissa are efforts to foster connectivity, accessibility to services and information dissemination to people.

DECENTRALISED GOVERNANCE

The first generation of development had 'growth' as its central theme. The developing countries replicated the models, programmes, and projects of the developed nations. Importance was given to the concepts of industrialisation and modernisation. This optimism receded when it was realised in the '70s and '80s that development was not able to remove poverty and inequality. The reason was that development did not address the issues of equity. Development administration was not participative, responsive and accessible. No attention was given to the development of the poor. Hence, there was a need to redirect development efforts towards the poor and those at the grassroots. Development was to address the priorities of the masses, especially the poor, and the efforts made were to be sustainable, efficient and equitable.

Decentralisation addresses the question of sustainable, efficient and equitable development through improvement in service delivery by targeting the beneficiaries, identifying their needs, enabling their participation and delivering and satisfying their needs. Decentralisation should be seen as a theory of development, which requires a variety of institutions for empowering and uplifting the marginalised and the poor. The PRIs, the private sector, and the civil society organisations, all play an important role in decentralised governance. A new framework of decentralised governance for the society can be laid down by taking the following measure:

1. Providing people the opportunities and the forums to articulate their views and perceptions which can be expressed in future policies, thus enabling them to participate in the formulation of policies.
2. Taking the points of service delivery closer to the people.
3. Strengthening the local bodies as units of self-government.

Decentralised governance seeks to tap local initiatives and practices by involving grassroots organisations such as self-help groups. Collective efforts are thus articulated. Decentralisation leads to the empowerment of the local people through deconcentration and devolution. Deconcentration brings service delivery closer to people through field agencies. Devolution redistributes power to the local communities via local bodies and enables them to participate in the policies affecting them. Thus, both representative democracy and participatory democracy become possible. Decentralised governance is therefore an alternative strategy of development, which is people-centred, participatory and bottom-up. It fosters power redistribution, power redefinition and power relocation.

The 73rd and 74th constitutional amendments in 1992, have been major steps in this direction. They made development people-centred and regionally relevant. The amendments aimed at creating member-accountable institutions and provided the control and ownership of the resources to the people. For the first time, self-government is located at the *panchayat* level. Locality has become the basis of planning. The *gram panchayat* is entrusted with the responsibility for planning which is done by the people. The 73rd amendment provides for decentralised governance at the district and even lower levels. It has created people-centred institutions at the district, block and village level. The *panchayats* are to be directly elected from the territorial constituencies for a period of five years. The state election commission is responsible for conducting the elections. The state finance commission is to review the finances of the *panchayats* and it recommends the taxes to be assigned to the various tiers. Thus, *panchayats* are responsible for the planning and implementation of programmes related to social justice and economic development.

There are over two million elected members of rural local bodies and about 60,000 in urban/municipal governments. State election commissions and state finance commissions have been set up. With the setting up of finance commissions and election commissions in the states, there is considerable degree of financial discipline, cost consciousness, transparency, resource mobilisation, and regular elections.

However, there are certain constraints in the operation of this decentralised pattern of governance. The states can dissolve rural local bodies without giving them a reasonable opportunity of being heard before such dissolution. The eleventh schedule of the constitution assigns the same type of responsibilities to all the three tiers at the *panchayat* level. Thus, there is overlapping of jurisdiction. There is no attempt to differentiate the levels of responsibilities as per the organisation and finances of these bodies. This creates problems in determining the basis of distribution of resources by the finance commission in favour of each level. Local level planning is also not effective, as it is mostly the state's planning priorities and sectoral allocations that have the decisive force. Local planning has to be linked with local resource mobilisation and should involve the support of the local people.

Local self-government is one way to operationalise decentralisation. Decentralisation also becomes effective by the privatisation of certain public services, such as, health, insurance, telecommunications, transport and infrastructure development such as construction of bridges, highways, roads, dams, etc. The role of the state may be that of a producer, deliverer, licensor, contractor, financier or regulator. For each of the services, the government will have to assess which of these roles are appropriate. Mechanisms to monitor, control, and regulate pricing and management of parallel markets of publicly and privately produced or delivered services have to be laid down (Tandon et al).

Another feature of decentralised governance is interactive policy making which leads to decentralised decision-making. Interactive policy can be defined as a process to form a common conception towards a collective policy practice in a network of mutually dependent participants (Bekkers quoted in Monique Esselbrugge). The government and non-governmental actors—the private sector, non-governmental organisations (NGOs), communities, grassroots organisations, pressure groups, all participate in decision-making so as to influence issues and suggest alternatives. They become co-makers of decisions. The actors participate in expressing problems and generating solutions, thus arriving at a common alternative. The knowledge of and inputs from various actors enrich the policy and enhance its quality and legitimacy. It also makes the policy include the growing diversity, dynamics and complexity of social issues (Scharpf and Klijn quoted in Monique Esselbrugge), thus enabling it to address social issues better and bridge the gap between government and society. Interactive policy making may sometimes lead to certain pressures from a variety of actors, each having its own perceptions, interests, claims, knowledge and resources that have to be accommodated.

ISSUES AND STRATEGIES IN GOVERNANCE OF PUBLIC SERVICE DELIVERY

The issues and strategies in governance of public service delivery discussed above, are dealt within the chapters of this book.

The development and reforms in good governance in India, according to the connotations given by the World Bank, Organization for Economic Cooperation and Development (OECD) and other agencies, have been dealt with in the second chapter. Beginning with the concept of good governance given by Kautilya in ancient times, the chapter details the current definitions, determinants and components of good governance. The role of the state has undergone a redefinition. New organs such as the private sector and the civil society have called for such a redefinition. The state, through its formal agencies encourages the private sector and civil society to participate in governance. The goal of the state, private sector and civil society should be to attain sustainable human development by establishing the political, legal, economic and social circumstances for poverty reduction, job creation, advancement of women and environmental protection. The Indian government has come out with different reform measures, especially since 1991. The New Economic Policy, the opening up of the public sector, decentralised local governance by way of the 73rd and 74th amendments, the involvement of civil society groups in decision-making, and the IT Act, 2000, depict the implementation of good governance in India.

The third chapter highlights the issues and strategies of governance for development. There are three areas of focus for governance—empowering people with skills that would enable them to contribute to the economy and society, facilitating the economy and the market and regulating the environment in a transparent manner. Governance will be effective if suitable strategies are devised for the same. Dissemination of accurate and timely information, and interaction with the public is a key factor for quality governance. IT localisation will go a long way in reaching the masses and empowering people. Citizens have the right to seek information pertaining to matters of interest. Likewise, IT will also facilitate the working of the economy and the market. The Internet, World Wide Web, teleconference and e-mail have enabled the functioning of economies. Computer penetration, at an affordable cost and training centres in villages, schools, government and business establishments are necessary. Similarly, television, as a means of communication and information can be used to reach out to people. Language networking that facilitates the exchange of communication is essential. The budget and government rules and regulations need to be made public. There is a need to generate more IT manpower. Efforts are being made by the Government of India with the Massachusetts Institute of Technology (MIT), to bring the benefits of the most sophisticated and emerging technologies to alleviate the problems of the poor and the least educated in the country, and enhancing relations between organisations in India and research groups at MIT. Attempts have been made by states like Andhra Pradesh, Madhya Pradesh and Karnataka to use ICT in public service delivery. Educational institutions like the Indira Gandhi National Open University are using technology to empower the disadvantaged.

The issues in good governance can be addressed better by bringing in changes in the style and functioning of the government machinery, including the bureaucracy; and the law and order machinery, including the judicial system. The fourth chapter deals with the first part and suggests a transformative agenda for the bureaucracy. The government machinery needs to be made more transparent, accountable, responsive and participatory. Governance reforms aim at creating partnerships, interactive policy making and network management, thus involving different actors in policy making. Bureaucracy has to transform itself to accommodate this and at the same time function within the networks of interdependent actors. A hierarchical mechanism does not cope well with this change. Bureaucracy has to change and establish a fruitful partnership among various actors—government, private and civil society groups to coordinate their activities. Bureaucracy has to work under political direction and adhere to professional standards in policy formulation and implementation. Likewise, policy makers have to lessen political control and provide political direction and tempo for civil service reforms. This will make the bureaucracy flexible, open and less susceptible to political pressures, which in turn will develop new routines, organisational concepts and skills such as democratising administration, generating managerial consciousness, reducing paperwork and secrecy, adapting new technologies, and training in ethics. This will enable it to strengthen the efforts of individuals and groups in the society and involve them in policies and decisions affecting them. This will also enable the bureaucracy to act as a catalyst and an interface between the elected officials and society.

The fifth chapter emphasises the need for a change in the style and functioning of the law and order machinery, including the judicial system. It deals with responsive administration of the criminal justice system in India. Four main issues related to criminal justice are addressed. These are—the making of laws, the enforcement of laws by the police, trials by judicial courts and jails. To enable the criminal justice system to be responsive to changes in present day governance, there is need to modify the rational method of making a brief law, modernise the police, set a grievance redressal machinery, identify the causes of delay, devise possible methods of expediting quick and clear decisions, and introducing summary trials, mobile courts and village courts.

Chapters five and six give a detailed treatment to the new opportunities offered by e-governance to enable the government reach people and make it possible for them to participate in governance. It not only empowers people with the right to information, but also helps the government machinery to change its style and functioning. Thus, e-governance lays down a new vision for governance. Chapter six focuses on the four models of e-governance, which provide opportunity and scope for improvement in governance. The General Dissemination Model disseminates the government information already in the public domain to a wider public domain through the application of information technology. This includes the publication of government laws, names and addresses of officials and the performance of the government on the Internet. This enhances interaction between the people and administration. The second model, i.e. Critical Information Dissemination Model is restricted to the dissemination of critical information to a targeted audience or to a wider public domain. This includes publishing corruption cases, research studies, human rights violation, environmental issues, etc. This promotes information-based decision-making and action, either by a specific group of the population or by the people at large, and fosters public opinion or debate. The third model, i.e. the Advocacy Model, as the name suggests, advocates the civil society's influence on decision-making by forming virtual communities or specific groups within as well as outside the government. The model thus mobilises concerted action on pertinent issues facing the community. The fourth model is the Interactive Service Model, which is the consolidation of the other three models. This model provides for two-way information flow. This leads to greater participation, efficiency and transparency. Some areas of application of this model are—elections, grievance redressal, decentralised governance, opinion polls, etc. All these models, thus, help people to participate in one form or the other in matters affecting them.

Chapter seven deals with the significant areas of e-governance, such as—education, rural development, industry, passport matters, registration of vehicles, driving license, police, customs, and payment of taxes and bills. An electronic 'citizen identity card' should be provided to every citizen. This card should be used to avail government assistance, for voting, as a driving license and for availing subsidised food through the public distribution system.

Different states in India have initiated various ICT based programmes and projects. These initiatives rest on connectivity and networking of various services and departments. With the Internet citizens are able to gain access to the information they need. Such initiatives are generally based on public-private partnership and involve cost and revenue sharing with the private sector. There is more accountability due to multiple stakeholders. Chapter eight covers the ICT initiative, namely project Saukaryam, in Visakhapatnam. The various activities of the project include data collection, computerisation, networking, providing civic services online and establishment of call centres as outlets for citizens to access the services. The civic services include online payment of municipal dues, getting birth and death certificates, application for building plan approval, lodging complaints/grievances and making other miscellaneous payments.

In chapter nine the e-governance initiatives taken in Chandigarh where a comprehensive IT policy was formulated in April 2000, are outlined. The aim of the policy was to provide public services, promote industry and business, reduce unemployment, increase software exports and improve the quality of life of the people through the use of ICT. The policy envisions improvements in the internal administration on the one hand, by facilitating budget preparation, providing connectivity between government departments, increasing the speed of file movement and enhancing the training of personnel. On the other hand, it aims to improve the citizen-government interface by providing information facilitation counters, computerisation of excise and taxation procedures, computerisation of educational institutions, municipal matters, issuance of licenses, registration of vehicles, police and setting up the city's website.

The concept of development and the importance of governance for development is highlighted in chapter ten. It also raises a number of governance issues that need to be resolved. These issues pertain to delayed decisions, complexity and comprehensiveness of government departments. The chapter suggests strategies to address these issues. These strategies include decentralisation, economic growth, public-private partnership and e-governance. ICT initiatives in Karnataka are highlighted. These initiatives can be classified into three categories. The first category deals with the interface between government and citizens. The second deals with improving human resources and connectivity, and the third aims to improve the efficiency of government officials.

The benefits of e-governance can be immediately made available to citizens in developing countries through computerised front-end interface for the common person to access public services, without waiting for backend computerisation. This has been the bottom line of the FRIENDS project, in Kerala, as discussed in chapter eleven. In Kerala, an IT enabled, single window, front-end interface has been set up for availing a range of popular public services like payment of taxes and utility charges and renewal of licenses, without waiting for back-end computerisation or systems integration in the government. Simple technologies can be creatively used to deliver services and starting from the front-end, optimal results can be achieved. Likewise, sharing of benefits and costs by participating departments has provided a network for effective disbursement of services.

Chapter twelve discusses the application of e-governance in various development areas in Orissa. The Gramsat Pilot Project undertaken by the Government of Orissa, addresses many aspects of governance, such as transparency, accountability, responsiveness, reduction of corruption, training and skill development, people's participation, disaster management, and project planning and monitoring. It will provide connectivity between the state capital, the districts and the blocks. Besides, communication nodes will also connect the *gram panchayats.* The project aims to create a master database containing information on geology, civic amenities, infrastructure, geography, Industries, motor vehicles, etc. The major application areas of the project will be interactive training, dissemination of development information to the people and grassroots functionaries, and MIS disaster warning, relief and rescue operations.

In chapter thirteen the ICT endeavours of Tamil Nadu have been detailed. The state has focused on ICT by computerising 206 blocks, 102 municipalities, and 6 corporations to provide various services including welfare services, entitled services, grievance redressal and public information to the people. Besides, by incorporating asset management software, the municipalities and corporations find it very easy to perform their functions such as the collection of property tax, water charges, professional tax, etc. Various departments like revenue, commercial taxes, electricity board, civil supplies, public distribution system, medical services, industries, education, public works have hosted websites containing information pertaining to them. Computerisation has also rendered automation in the internal functioning of departments.

Good governance entails power sharing by people in decision-making. Democratic decentralisation enables local governance in the sense that power gets devolved and deconcentrated. There is mobilisation of local support and utilisation of local resources for development. Likewise, there is reduction in decision-making levels, reduction in apathy of administration towards the clientele, and equity in allocation of resources and investments. Chapter fourteen deals with democratic, decentralised governance for rural development in Mizoram. While highlighting the provisions of the 73rd constitutional amendment a comparative study is made of the existing local government units—Autonomous District Councils and Village Councils—with the *panchayati raj* system. The chapter synthesises the positive thrusts of both and suggests that while certain provisions of the 73rd amendment should be incorporated in the state, the unique characteristics of tribal societies and tribal areas have also to be kept in mind.

Decentralised governance aims to tap the local initiatives at the grassroots level. Such an effort of self-help is depicted in chapter fifteen which examines the case of a village called Sukhomajri in Haryana, where self- help groups have contributed to better the lives of the people in the village through participatory natural resource management. The Sukhomajri Watershed Management Project was started to protect the catchment area of the dams built across Lake Sukhna. The management of the project was given to a society formed by the villagers, namely the Hill Resources Management Society. The society consists of the head of every village family and aims at protection of hilly areas from grazing and illicit felling of trees, distribution of irrigation water from dams on payment basis, and maintenance of dams, water and other assets. This has resulted in an increase in the income of people and has rejuvenated local governance through self-help.

REFERENCES

1. Tandon, B.B., V.K. Agnihotri and H. Ramachandran, 'Globalization and decentralization: Emerging issues from the Indian experience', *International Review of Administrative Sciences*, Vol. 67, No. 3, Sage Publications, New Delhi, 2001.
2. Heeks, R. and David Mundy, 'Information systems and public sector reform in the third world', *The Internationalization of Public Management,* (Eds.) Willy McCourt and Martin Minogue, Edward Elgar, UK, 2000.
3. McCourt, W. and Martin Minogue, 'The internationalization of public management—reinventing the third world state', *New Horizons of Public Policy Series*, (Eds.) Edward Elgar, UK, 2001.
4. Denhardt, R.B. and J.V. Denhardt, 'The new public service: Serving rather than steering', *Public Administrative Review*, Vol. 60, No. 6, Nov.–Dec., 2000.
5. Bekkers, V.J.J.M., 'Information and communication technology and the redefinition of the functional and normative boundaries of government', *Governance in Modern Society*, (Eds.) Oscar Van Heffen et al., Kluwer Academic Publishers, Netherlands, 2000.
6. Klijn, E.H. and Geert R. Teisman, 'Managing public private partnerships: influencing processes and institutional context of public private partnerships', *Governance in Modern Society*, (Eds.)

Oscar Van Heffen et al., Kluwer Academic Publishers, Netherlands, 2000.

7. McCourt, W., 'The NPM agenda for service delivery: A suitable model for developing countries?' *The Internationalization of Public Management*, (Eds.) Willy McCourt and Martin Minogue, Edward Elgar, UK, 2000.
8. Commonwealth Secretariat, 'Introducing new approaches: Improved public service delivery', *Managing the Public Service: Strategies for Improvement Series*, No. 5, 1998.
9. Esselbrugge, M., 'Interactive policy making as a serious alternative: Balancing between an open and closed approach', *Governance in Modern Society*, (Eds.) Oscar Van Heffen et al., Kluwer Academic Publishers, Netherlands, 2000.
10. Kernaghan, K. 'The post-bureaucratic organisation and public service values', *International Review of Administrative Sciences*, Vol. 66, No. 1, Sage Publications, New Delhi, 2000.
11. Bhattacharya, M., *New Horizons of Public Administration*, Jawahar Publishers, New Delhi, 1998.
12. Minocha, O.P., 'Good governance: New public management perspective', *The Indian Journal of Public Administration*, IIPA, Vol. XLIV, No. 3, July–Sept., New Delhi, 1998.
13. Mukhopadhyay, A., 'Reinventing government for good governance', *The Indian Journal of Public Administration*, IIPA, Vol. XLIV, No. 3, July–Sept., New Delhi, 1998.
14. Sharma, A.K., 'People's empowerment', *The Indian Journal of Public Administration*, IIPA, Vol. XLII, No. 3, July–Sept., New Delhi, 1996.

2

Development and Reforms in Good Governance with Special Reference to India

— E. Vayunandan

INTRODUCTION

Good governance, since ancient times, has been conceptualised as an ideal state or *Rama Rajya*. This notion endures even now, as good governance is seen to bring in happiness and welfare of the people. It is also associated with efficient and effective administration in a democratic framework. As such, administration should be development oriented and committed to the people.

Kautilya in his treatise *Arthashastra* elaborated the traits of the King of a good governance state as, "in the happiness of his subjects, lies his happiness; in their welfare, his welfare; whatever pleases himself, he does not consider as good, but whatever pleases his subjects he considers as good" (Sharma, L.N. and Susmita Sharma, 1998). Plato is credited with developing the concept of the *Philosopher King* as the ideal ruler. Aristotle was perhaps the first political theorist to deal with the term 'governance' when he classified political organisations by indicating the manner in which they were ruled—a kind of numerical court of rule by one (dictatorship), a few (autocracy), or many (democracy) (Sinclair, 1962).

In its simple dictionary meaning, *good governance* refers to the well-being of people. The Oxford dictionary defines governance as the act or manner of governing, or the way of control. Governance lends itself to a wider meaning, which includes the processes as well as the results of making authoritative decisions for the benefit of the society. It is more comprehensive in meaning and implications than the word government. Government refers to the machinery and institutional arrangements of exercising sovereign power for serving the internal and external interests of the 'political community', whereas governance means making policies for the development of organisations as well as people. Today, good governance has entered the development lexicon, where the focus has shifted from 'maximising the quality of development funding to maximising of development outcomes and effectiveness of public service delivery' (*Mid Term Appraisal of 9th Five Year Plan*).

Good governance and its basic determinants have been defined by various scholars, international agencies and reports. We will now discuss these.

DEVELOPMENT OF GOOD GOVERNANCE

Governance has existed since ancient times. Kautilya in the *Arthashastra* emphasises that in the pursuit of good governance, the King was to govern for the welfare of the people.

Kautilya mentions the following ten imperatives of good governance for a King (Sharmasastry, R. 1929):

1. Merge his individuality with his duties
2. Guide administration
3. Avoid extremes without missing the goal
4. Lead a disciplined life with a code of conduct
5. Pay fixed salaries and allowances
6. Maintain law and order
7. Stress on *lekhaks* (writers)
8. Carry out preventive/punitive measures against corrupt officials
9. Replace bad ministers by good ones
10. Emulate administrative qualities

The World Bank Prescription

In recent years, the concept of good governance has received heightened impetus by multilateral and bilateral aid-giving agencies as a pre-condition for providing aid. In this context, in 1989, the World Bank in its documents on sub-Saharan Africa mentioned four key dimensions of good governance: (i) public sector management, (ii) accountability, (iii) legal framework for development and (iv) information and transparency. According to the document, 'Improving governance would begin with an assessment of the institutional environment which determines the patrimonial profile of the country—high when all other factors are absent and low when they are present'. Thus, good governance has to focus on accountability, rule of law, openness and transparency.

Further, the World Bank in its document, *Governance and Development* (1992) defined governance as 'the manner in which power is exercised in the management of a country's economic and social resources for development'. The bank came to realise that 'good governance is central to creating and sustaining an environment which fosters strong and equitable development, and it is an essential complement to sound economic policies'. It identified the following three distinctive aspects of good governance:

1. The form of the political regime (military or civil, parliamentary or presidential, authoritative or democratic).
2. The process by which authority is exercised in the management of a country's economic and social resources for development.
3. The capacity of governments to design, formulate and implement policies, and to discharge government functions.

Organisation for Economic Cooperation and Development (OECD)

"The concept of governance denotes the use of political authority and exercise of control in a society in relation to the management of its resources for social and economic development". The OECD lays down the following three-fold role for public authorities:

1. Establishing the environment in which economic operators functions.
2. Determining the distribution of benefits.
3. Deciding the nature of the relationship between the ruler and the ruled.

The key components of governance identified by OECD are as follows:

(a) Legitimacy of government.
(b) Accountability of political and official elements of government.
(c) Competence of governments to make policy and deliver services.
(d) Respect for human rights and the rule of law.

Commission on Global Governance

The Commission, in 1995, considered governance as the totality of management of affairs by individuals and the public and private institutions affecting them. 'It is a continuing process through which conflicting or diverse interests may be accommodated and cooperative action may be taken'. This is made possible through formal institutions and informal arrangements of the people and their institutions.

Habitat II Conference

The Habitat II Conference held in Istanbul in June 1996, identified the following characteristics of good governance:

1. Accountability
2. Transparency
3. Participation
4. Rule of law
5. Partnership of public and private institutions (United Nations Center for Human Settlements, 1996).

United Nations Development Programme (UNDP)

Governance is viewed as the exercise of economic, political and administrative authority to manage a country's affairs at all levels. It comprises mechanisms, processes, and institutions, through which citizens and groups can articulate their interests, exercise their legal rights, meet their obligations, and mediate their differences (United Nations Development Programme, 1997).

The characteristics of good governance, laid down by UNDP, are as follows:

1. Participation
2. Rule of law
3. Transparency
4. Responsiveness
5. Consensus orientation
6. Equity
7. Effectiveness and efficiency
8. Accountability
9. Strategic vision

United Nations Educational, Scientific and Cultural Organisation (UNESCO)

UNESCO lays emphasis on making citizens contribute to the positive social and economic development of society. It defines governance as, a political process that encompasses the whole society and contributes to the making of citizens, active contributors to the social contract that binds them together. Their sense of political efficacy is one of the indicators of democratic governance.

Report on Human Development in South Asia

This report, more than any other, focusses on human governance. It defines human governance as good governance dedicated to secure human development. It requires effective participation of people in state, civil society, and private sector activities that are conducive to human development. Human governance must lead to broad-based economic growth and social development which in turn would bring about greater human development. Governance must be seen by the people as operating in their interests only—transparent and accountable to all its constituents, and conducive to building a society in which all believe they are treated fairly and decently.

The report conceptualises three dimensions of governance, conducive for human development—political governance, economic governance and civil governance.

Political Governance

The characteristics of political governance are:

- Rule of law
- Accountability
- Transparency
- No frequent amendment of the constitution
- Free and fair multi-party elections
- Clear separation of powers

Economic Governance

The following are the implications of economic governance:

- Macro-economic stability
- Guaranteeing property rights
- Removing market distortions
- Eliminating rent-seeking opportunities
- Investment in people and basic infrastructure
- Protection of natural environment
- Progressive and equitable fiscal system to promote economic growth with social justice.

Civil Governance

- securing fundamental political, economic and human rights;
- empowering and protecting women, the poor, ethnic and religious minorities.

From the preceding discussion, we can deduce that governance is of a dynamic and moving nature. On the whole, it implies the following:

- Management of the affairs of the state for the well-being of citizens.
- Delivering to every citizen, the rights as laid down in the country's constitution.
- Enhancing the political, social and economic life of every citizen.
- Institutionalised system of governance.
- Ensuing transparent, responsive, responsible, accountable, action-oriented, ethical and accessible form of governance.

REDEFINITION OF THE STATE IN THE CONTEXT OF GOOD GOVERNANCE

The characteristic features of good governance, defined in the preceding paragraphs, compel a redefinition and reinvention of the state. State, since ancient times, performed all functions pertaining to law and order, development, and protection of the country's sovereignty. Gradually it became a leviathan. It became burdened with all these functions, which grew in density and scope with time. As a result, the state was unable to perform all these activities. This resulted in neglect of certain vital issues, related to the social and economic development of the country. The administration operated as a watertight compartment, inaccessible and irresponsive to the people. Such governance cannot flourish in the present era of governance reforms. The State has to be redefined in the context of all these. Hasnat Abdul Hye, in a recent work, writes:

> Traditionally State has been defined as composed of only three official components—Parliament, Judiciary and Executive. The local government bodies, private sector and the civil society have been considered as the external components of the state mechanism. Local bodies, private sector and civil society, on their part, either existed in their inchoate conditions or were considered to be simply non-existent at that stage. But the point is that the relative position of the different organs of the state changed with the passage of time and as a dependent variable of different crosscutting factors, the development of the 'informal' organs of the state gained impetus when the state through its formal agencies encouraged the private sector and the civil society to participate in governance. This process gives rise to new 'organs' of the state in terms of their social acceptance, autonomy and the resources which call for a redefinition of the state itself. So redefined governance arises in place of the traditional governance either because of deliberate politics pursued by the state in an evolutionary way or through an increasingly vibrant private sector and an expanding civil society including NGOs and other agencies as well.

Hasnat Abdul Hye has presented schematically, the comparison between the traditional and redefined state (Figure 1.1).

The main role of the redefined state should be sustainable human development with contributions from civil societies and the private sector. Sustainable human development will ensure the following:

1. Empowerment of people by increasing their opportunities to participate in making decisions that affect them and in exercising their choices.
2. Cooperation, whereby people will work together for their well-being.
3. Equity, ensuing equal access to public services.
4. Sustainability, providing sensitivity to environmental resources.
5. Security, engendering safe, harmonious and conducive living.

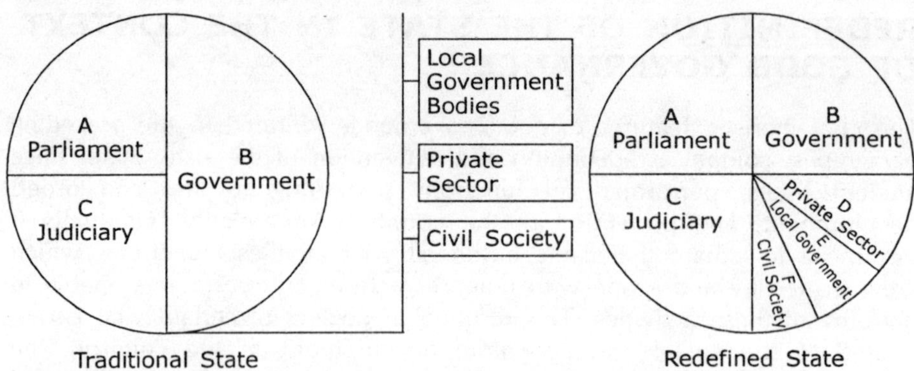

FIGURE 2.1 Comparison between the traditional and the redefined state.

GOVERNANCE IN THE INDIAN CONTEXT

Democracy provides citizens with a government, to satisfy their needs and aspirations. The Government of India has been alive to these needs since Independence and has been taking various measures to bring in administrative reforms. The state is to be an efficient provider of basic services, public goods and a facilitator for economic growth in the light of globalisation. Administration has to re-orient itself to function in the changed context. Some recent developments that have led to various measures taken by the government are:

1. Opening up of the Indian economy
2. Decentralisation and democratic empowerment at the grassroots
3. Administrative reforms
4. Information technology

These measures are discussed as follows.

New Economic Policy, 1991

In India, the state has played an important role in the country's economy leading to rapid industrialisation. However, due to a multiplicity of objectives, the state failed to provide reasonable surplus. This resulted in adverse balance of payments, rising national debts and problems in the public sector. To mitigate these adverse economic consequences, there emerged a consensus that the state needed to be rolled back. This was also emphasised by international agencies like the World Bank and the International Monetary Fund (IMF).

The New Economic Policy, 1991, reduced the scope and role of the public sector. The focus was on creating conditions whereby the public sector could function in competition with the private sector. The government is trying to achieve these objectives by deregulating industries and liberalising foreign investment and technological imports. Now, only eight types of industries, of security and strategic concern, are with the public sector, which is to invest only in infrastructure and in the protection of the poorest.

Various steps have been taken to protect consumers. The Monopolies and Restrictive Trade Practices Act (MRTP), which aims to prevent and control monopolistic, restrictive and unfair trade practices has been amended. Likewise, steps have been taken to disinvest equities of selected public sector units through financial institutions and mutual funds to raise finance for development. The government has acquired a more promotional role to provide a conducive environment for the public and the private sector.

Decentralised Governance

Grassroots governance has been a major concern of the planning process in India ever since the introduction of *panchayati raj* in 1959. While the introduction of the system was a landmark in the history of administrative reforms, the follow-up action in different states failed to provide it with positive direction, particularly, in the realm of development administration. The spirit of democratic decentralisation that evolved over the years is being practiced only in a limited way and has not experienced wholesome sustainability. It was probably this state of affairs, which paved the way for a crucial national agenda on *panchayati raj* reforms, culminating in the 73rd Constitutional Amendment (Jain, 1999).

This amendment aims at integrating the concept of people's participation in a formal way with the planning process on the one hand and the devolution of responsibility to the people themselves on the other. In 1996, through Central Act 40, the provision of *panchayats* has been extended to Scheduled Areas (traditional tribal areas). These Acts have addressed the persistent problems of irregular elections, supersessions, inadequate representation, insufficient devolution of powers and lack of administrative and financial autonomy and inadequate resources.

Several initiatives have been made by non-governmental organsations (NGOs) to involve local communities in managing their own affairs. Many state governments have launched schemes and programmes to promote people's participation. The guidelines of several centrally-sponsored schemes helped community based organisations (CBOs) to formulate and implement development programmes. Among the central ministries, remarkable steps have been taken by the ministries of rural development (e.g. watershed associations, watershed committees, users groups under DPAP, DDP and IWDP), environment and forests (e.g. joint forest management), education (e.g. village education committees under DPEP) and water resources (participatory water management through water users associations/committees). These experiences have increased the transparency and accountability of the state.

Administrative Reforms

The Government of India organised a Conference of Chief Secretaries of States and Union Territories on November 20, 1996, focusing on accountable, open and citizen-friendly government, improving performance and integrity of functionaries, initiating corrective steps to arrest the present drift in management of public services and restoring people's faith in the fairness, integrity and responsiveness of the administration. This was followed by a Conference of Chief Ministers on May 24, 1997, which concluded that governance has to extend beyond conventional bureaucracies and actively involve citizens and consumer groups at all levels, empower and inform the public and the disadvantaged groups so as to ensure service delivery and programme execution through autonomous, elected local bodies. The conference also proposed to set up new autonomous regulatory agencies with quasi-judicial powers to ensure that the functioning of private units is regulated in social interests.

The conference came out with an action plan dealing with the following three themes:

1. Accountable and citizen-friendly government

(i) Providing citizen's charters
(ii) Redressal of public grievances
(iii) Review of laws, regulations and procedures
(iv) People's participation, decentralisation and devolution of powers

2. Transparency and right to information

(i) Easy access of people to all information relating to government activities
(ii) Introducing a legislation for freedom of information
(iii) Opening of computerised information and facilitation counters

3. Improving the performance and integrity of public services

(i) Code of ethics for civil services
(ii) Strengthening investigative agencies and the vigilance machinery
(iii) Strengthening various agencies like the Lok Ayukta, the CBI, the vigilance machinery, income tax authorities, Enforcement Directorate and the Comptroller and Auditor General (CAG)
(iv) Ensuring stability of tenure and depolitising postings at all levels

The central government and most of state governments have already taken steps in this direction.

Information Technology

The Information Technology Revolution Act, 2000, enables the application of information and communication technology (ICT) in governance—political, economic and social. E-governance or electronic governance has facilitated computerisation and networking of varied departments and also the delivery of public services. Networking has rendered the facilities of the Internet and the World Wide Web. This has led to connectivity among various government departments. Now these departments set up their own websites and upload information. Similarly, departments can coordinate with one another without much wastage of time. Computerisation of internal administration has rendered automation and improvement in record keeping and file movement.

Citizen centric services are now also rendered online. Various state governments have come up with projects and programmes, enabling the online rendering of services such as education, medical and health, police, agriculture and extension, employment, passport, registration of vehicles, birth and death certificates, filing of returns, and so forth.

CONCLUSION

The 1999 Report on Human Development in South Asia poses the following questions to the system of governance:

1. Do people fully participate in governance?
2. Are people fully informed?
3. Do people make decisions, or can they at least hold the decision-makers accountable?
4. Are women equal partners with men in governance?
5. Are the needs of the poor and disadvantaged met?
6. Are people's human rights guaranteed?
7. Are the needs of future generations taken into account in current policies?
8. Do people own their structures of governance?

The report lays down the following aspects for South Asian countries to pursue:

Firstly, they need to redirect their priorities towards the core human development concerns, viz. basic human needs of the poor, provision of efficiently targeted social safety nets and major redistribution of such productive assets such as land and credit.

Secondly, there is a need for revitalising existing state institutions by fair representation to all sections, represented and well-paid civil services, and independent and accessible judiciary.

Thirdly, new partnerships between the state and society have to be forged for any major turnaround, viz. government must provide a supportive framework to aid meaningful civil society initiatives and private sector enterprises.

Lastly, provide people with the right to information.

The success of governance depends on the reinvention of the government, re-engineering of the bureaucracy and the re-invigoration of non-government sectors, with a social motive. There is also need to have political will, normative concerns and organisational flexibility. The state, the private sector and the non-governmental organisations, especially the community based organisations should cooperate and coordinate with each other to make good governance possible.

REFERENCES

1. Aziz, Abdul and David D. Arnold (Eds.), *Decentralised Governance in Asian Countries*, Sage Publications, New Delhi, 1996.
2. Mukhopadhyay, Ashok, 'Reinventing government for good governance', *Indian Journal of Public Administration,* Vol. XLIV, No. 3, July–Sept., 1998.
3. Barker, James Jr., Bernard Tenenbaum and Fiona Woolf, "Governance and regulation of power pools and system operators; an international comparision', *The World Bank*, Washington, D.C., 1997.
4. Chopra, S.K. (Ed.), *Towards Good Governance*, Konark, Delhi, 1997.
5. 'Commission on global governance', *Our Global Neighbourhood,* Oxford University Press, New York, 1995.
6. Commonwealth Secretariat, 'Current good practices and new developments in public service management: a profile of the public service of Trinidad and Tobago', *Zimbabwe, Commonwealth Secretariat*, London, 1995–1997.
7. Osborne, David and Ted Gaebler, 'Reinventing government: How the entrepreneurial sprit is transforming public sector', Prenctice-Hall, New Delhi, 1992.
8. Government of India, 'An Agenda for Effective and Responsive Administration', *Ministry of Personnel*, Public Grievances and Pensions, New Delhi, November, 1996.
9. Asmerom, H.K., K. Borgman and R. Hoppe, 'Good governance, decentralisation and democratisation in post-colonial state', *Indian Journal of Public Administration*, Vol. 41, No. 4, Oct.–Dec., 1995.
10. Hye Hasnat Abdul, *Governance, South Asian Perspectives,* Manohar Publishers, New Delhi, 2001.
11. Jayaswal K.P., 'Hindu Polity', Bangalore Printing and Publishing Co., Bangalore, 1968.
12. Bhattacharya, Mohit, 'Conceptualising good governance', *Indian Journal of Public Administration,* Vol. XLIV, No. 3, July–Sept., 1998.

13. Minocha, O.P., 'Good governance: Concept and operational issues, management in government', 29(3), Oct.–Dec., 1997.

14. Minocha, O.P., 'Good governance: New public management perspective', *Indian Journal of Public Administration*, Vol. XLIV, No. 3, July–Sept., 1998.

15. Overseas Development Administration (ODA), *Taking Account of Good Government*, London, 1993.

16. Peter, Blunt, 'Cultural Relativism, Good Governance and Sustainable Human Development', *Public Administration and Development*, Vol. 15(1), 1995.

17. Sharmasastry, R., *Kautilya's Arthashastra*, Weslevan Mission Press, Mysore, 1929.

18. 'Towards good governance', *Indian Journal of Public Administration*, Vol. XLIV, No. 3, July–Sept., 1998.

19. The World Bank, World Development Report, *The State in a Changing World*, Oxford University Press, Oxford, 1997.

20. Kumar, Umesh, *Kautilya's thought on Public Administration*, National Book Organisation, Delhi, 1997.

21. UNCHS (1996), 'An urbanizing world: Global report on human settlements', *United Nations Centre for Human Settlement (HABITAT)*, New York, Oxford, 1996.

22. UNDP, *A UNDP Policy Paper: Strategy on Governance*, (draft paper), New York, 1997.

23. World Bank, *Governance and Development*, World Bank Publications, Washington, D.C., 1992.

24. World Bank, *Governance: The World Bank's Experience*, World Bank Publication, Washington, D.C., 1994.

25. World Bank, *Managing Development: The governance dimension*, World Bank Publications, Washington, D.C., 1991..

26. Human Development Report in South Asia, The crisis of governance, human development centre, OUP, 1999, Karachi, Pakistan.

3

Governance for Development: Issues and Strategies

— D.K. Ghosh

INTRODUCTION

Fundamentally, the word 'governance', in relation to a country, means offering the people a system, competent to provide various facilities for a quality life that also needs security. And since a democratic government is of the people, by the people and for the people, wherein all roles are performed by citizens, directly or indirectly, government regulations and control have to be ultimately for the good of the people. Thus, people are at the root and they are the ultimate too. Governance also means 'control' and 'authority'. Wherever control and authority are necessary, they should be exercised keeping in mind, the interests of people. Good governance entails sustainable economic and social development that draws upon adequate infrastructure.

GOVERNANCE AND DEVELOPMENT

Development is the objective and governance, the mechanism or means. In view of this, we need to see which are the various factors that would contribute to the overall development of our country. Partial or incomplete development cannot, for obvious reasons, achieve the objectives of governance. As governance has to function through various systems and processes of the government machinery and private initiatives, the pre-requisite is that the machinery and the processes be good, flexible, sound, efficient, cost-effective and objective in approach. A nation's governance plays the most important role in shaping the destiny of its people. Weak governance and slow economic development go hand-in-hand, observed the International Monetary Fund (IMF). Within India, some of 'the most prosperous regions have a history of having better governance', observes the IMF.

Good governance would improve the management of public resources, like the government treasury, the central bank (the Reserve Bank of India in our case), public sector enterprises, revenue and expenditure, public distribution system, law and order machinery, and the overall administrative machinery. Since the failure of the socialist economies, the thrust is on the role of the private sector. This stems from the realisation that entrepreneurial capabilities are basic to individuals and organisations, and cannot be replicated by a single entity i.e., the government. Some of the biggest capitalist economies of the world have raised the standards of living of their people by using the entrepreneurial abilities of individuals and organisations, and raised more revenues for the governments, which would enable them to administer even better. Most communist countries are also doing just that. This focus requires the government to develop and maintain a regulatory environment that is conducive to efficient private sector activities. Creation of physical and human infrastructure that would facilitate continuous and sustainable economic and social development by entrepreneurs in the society is a must for good governance.

ISSUES IN GOVERNANCE

Good governance is the cumulative result of a combination of factors such as superior management of government machinery and public resources on the one hand, and a regulatory environment conducive to efficient private sector activities on the other. For the latter, a better government would try to frame a policy of promoting private initiatives in various areas and at the same time, lay down the guiding principles, objectives and delivery system so people's interests are protected at all times. This presupposes a strong, efficient, responsive and sensitive government machinery empowered with modern facilities and mindset. Since the most challenging task before the government is to generate an environment for efficient functioning of various activities, the focus should be on: (i) empowering people with the skills that would enable them to contribute to the economy and society at large, (ii) facilitating the economy and markets, and (iii) regulating the environment in a transparent manner.

Empowering People with Skills to Make a Contribution

While communication technologies have thrown open enormous opportunities to the world, James D. Wolfenson, President, World Bank, in the foreword to the *World Development Report—Knowledge for Development 1998–99*, cautioned that 'these ... opportunities came with tremendous risks, that the globalisation of trade, finance and information flow is intensifying competition, raising the danger that the poorest countries and communities will fall behind more rapidly than ever before'. He wants us not to forget, in our enthusiasm for the information highway, the villages and slums without telephones, electricity and safe drinking water or the primary schools without blackboards, paper and books. All our efforts to raise the level of our people will fail if serious efforts are not made to take this fact into account as part of the development agenda.

In a knowledge based society, education is basic to all efforts toward peace and prosperity. While primary and secondary education is the foundation for higher education, the domain of higher education needs to be dwelt upon a little more. In a highly competitive world, following economic liberalisation and globalisation of the economy, creation and recreation of skilled manpower is the *sine qua non* to achieve the objectives of development. With the advent of IT, the complexion of manpower needs has dramatically changed beyond recognition due to market forces.

The Task Force on IT and Software Development, appointed by the Government of India, recommended, *inter alia,* Operation Knowledge to universalise computer literacy and to spread the use of computers and IT in education. It recommended, 'Computers and Internet should be available in every school, polytechnic, college, university and public hospital by 2003'. To achieve this, a beginning has to be made at the school level or ideally, even before schooling starts. In the USA, many children have some experience of computers either through games or through serious teaching programmes long before they enter school. In India also, similar things are happening, but they are generally limited to urban areas.

For optimal benefits in higher education, the Task Force also recommended that all institutions of higher education should be networked for distance education. Undeniably, empowering people is the most important factor in development. This can happen only through education and training. In the emerging world of competition, people have to be trained, not only in their own areas of specialisation, but also to be fully aware of the powers that lie in getting information so that they can exercise both their responsibilities and rights as citizens of India.

We have more than 12,000 colleges and about 250 universities and equivalent institutions with 80 lakh registered students. Generally, the facilities for computer education available in the universities and colleges are not capable of providing the desired training. Till the end of March 2000, the University Grants Commission (UGC) had provided grants for setting up computer centres in 130 universities and deemed universities. So far, the commission has provided support to only 3400 colleges out of about 12,000. However, during 1999–2000, the Commission paid Rs. 901.08 lakh to universities and colleges for establishing and augmenting computer facilities.

The Task Force on HRD in IT Manpower, appointed by the Ministry of Human Resource Development (MHRD) has made several positive recommendations to enable India to become a knowledge super power.

Among the various initiatives envisaged by MHRD are plans to optimally use the existing infrastructure of the IITs, RECs and other Engineering Colleges and educational institutions to double their student intake in IT in 2001–2002 and triple it in the next two years i.e., by 2003–2004. Besides, it is proposed to provide additional facilities to create more manpower in IT. When the various recommendations made in the report are implemented, they would go a long way in sustaining IT manpower development. However, as rightly pointed in the report, the major weakness in IT education, that will be aggravated by expansion of capacities is the non-availability of quality faculty. As the report says, this would be obvious '... due to heavy demand and better salaries and other perks offered by the industry'.

The 21st century will see the advent of a communication society facilitated by enormous progress in various fields: digitisation of information, storage power, information transfer technology (satellite networks and their coverage), international networking, development of virtual worlds, etc. The UNESCO working document on *Higher Education in the 21st Century: Vision and Action* observed that the advent of the communication society has many consequences for the world of work: decision-making is increasingly becoming remote from the areas of production, it can be carried out in real time thousands of kilometres away. IT makes different types of remote consultation (stock exchange, business-health indicators, lists of potential customers, lists of sub-contractors, price indexes, etc.) possible. Money no longer circulates in paper, but in virtual form; book-keeping is becoming increasingly delocalised; areas of production, distribution and research are becoming increasingly separate geographically but increasingly linked by new technology. IT has enabled more and more individuals to have simultaneous access to the same information, thus, shrinking the world into a *global village*. IT is also a vehicle for the internationalisation of culture and a tool for defending cultural identity; a major challenge to which higher education cannot remain indifferent.

In the process of people's empowerment, distance education can play a crucial role. This has been recognised all over the world. In India, the Indira Gandhi National Open University (IGNOU) offers distance educational programmes to its learners throughout the country. Currently, the university is offering 65 different undergraduate and postgraduate programmes to over 600,000 registered students from a cross-section of people in India. Not infrequently, comparisons are made between conventional face-to-face tuition and distance learning, which the Americans distinguish as synchronous and asynchronous learning. Thomas Russel, who has studied over 355 articles and papers about the effectiveness of distance learning in a paper called *The No Significant Difference Phenomenon* (Russel, 1999) suggests that there is no difference in the outcomes of students who study face-to-face, i.e. in conventional set-ups and students who study in distance education institutions. Even though his conclusion has been challenged by the Institute for Higher Education Policy (IHEP-1999), which says that the findings are flawed, the role of distance education institutions in IT education cannot be minimised.

E-governance

In the fast changing scenario, e-governance has become not only necessary but essential in a set-up where people are the biggest stakeholders. In this direction, the Union Ministry of Information Technology, has already made a number of initiatives, including the setting up of a centre for e-governance at the Massachusetts Institute of Technology (MIT), which will function as a forum for government officials, legislators, industry and various other key players to come together, discuss, learn and explore issues of shared importance.

Some of the objectives indicative of a road map for e-governance are as follows:

1. Develop a system for the seamless transfer of information between offices dealing with proper administration, both at the centre as well as in the states.
2. Set-up and/or facilitate specific communication networks for the government sector.
3. Assist central and state governments in identification and implementation of suitable hardware and software packages for e-governance.
4. Establish links worldwide with institutions engaged in similar activities so as to optimise synergies and benefits, by building/ sustaining platforms for interchange of ideas and experiences.
5. Develop special pilot projects on 'paperless government' online through an electric 'intelligent government' concept by extensive use of electronic forms and data entry interface through the use of the Web and Internet Technology.
6. Build convergence into connected services delivery programmes related to citizen devices.
7. Develop commercial and governmental systems for issuing and managing signatures/electronic signatures and smart cards.
8. Identify measures for suitable protection of data during filling up, transmission and alterations by using a combination of security measures.
9. Establish industry consultative committees (ICC), citizen consultative committees (CCC), ministries consultative committees (MCC) to provide a forum to various users, implementation groups and organisations to contribute towards the 25 per cent goal and beyond.

The e-government solution strongly supports digitisation of government administration by using *network technology* and *security technology* to meet the needs of both, the people providing services and those receiving them. As the Internet spreads throughout society, and in public as well as private sectors, operations such as e-applications and e-procurement become common place. Internet access is thus a pre-requisite to the e-government solution.

The Japanese Scenario

The Japanese government announced its Millennium Project in August 1999, aimed at realising the world's best e-government by 2003. It has already achieved a great deal in that direction. According to Hitachi Ltd., the most important factors in realising speedy government administration are instantaneousness via the Internet and high reliability in matters such as privacy protection. It has developed e-government solutions with the network technology and security technology in its core. The e-government solution developed by Hitachi offers the following four solutions.

1. **Government Service Infrastructure Solution** provides the infrastructure technology needed for digitisation of government administration, such as assurance of originality and authenticity, privacy protection, authentication and payment administration.
2. **Government Service Development Solution** supports development of various administrative services such as e-application, e-notification, e-procurement, information disclosure and document information management.
3. **Government Service Outsourcing Solution** provides proxy agencies for authentication centres.
4. **Government Service Consultation Solution** supports and evaluates government administration from the point of view of both system and business.

In order to educate people of all segments, in March 2000, Hitachi opened an e-government showroom in Shimbashi, Tokyo. This is Japan's first dedicated e-government showroom and has attracted over 5000 visitors, mainly from central and local government offices, within a year of its opening. At the showroom, people can see a demonstration of e-government systems and receive valuable information on products and infrastructure technologies that constitute the e-government solution.

Facilitating the Economy and Markets

The 20th century witnessed the innovation of mass assembly production which spread to various parts of the world; for example, Ford Motors of the United States of America, set up a factory in Argentina in the early part of the 20th century. The scale and spread of activities brought about by such type of production explosion also brought new management challenges. It was learned that to manage in the best possible manner, communication infrastructure was the best medium available to organisations. Earlier, different levels of managers appraised the progress of their units through phones, telex, fax and of late electronic communication systems like e-mails, tele-conferencing and video conferencing are widely used. The manageability thus provided, helps the functioning of big governments.

Big governments, introduced a large number of regulations required for the well-being of the people, in a magnitude never known or seen earlier. There was the unprecedented birth of large-scale public services. These public services, which ranged from tap water to employment exchanges, were funded by taxes. It is important to note that this achievement of governments was, to a large extent, supplemented by organised management and communication technology, never seen before. Now it is possible to access information and communicate easily just like businesses locate and interact with their suppliers. Little wonder then that General Motors based in the USA, acquires its parts from Sundaram Fastners in Chennai.

Many years after the first car assembly, commercial activities have become larger in scale and even more complex in technology and management. Markets seek higher efficiency and investors seek greater transparency. Information Technology is the facilitator this time. More and more businesses are extending their activities to the electronic media. This is popularly known as e-business or e-commerce. Managers monitor various activities through the various modes and processes of Information Technology. As we have noted earlier, the incredible development that the civilised world has seen in the 20th century, more particularly in its later half, rode on the back of efficient, pro-people governments and innovative enterprises.

The Singapore Scenario

The manner in which Singapore became the world's most efficient port, according to the *World Development Report*, is an example of having exploited the facility of electronic networking that made governance efficient and development-oriented. A networked information system functions through the Singapore Network Services (SNS), which enables traders to declare imports and exports for customs directly from their office computers. Trade net evolved from a five-person National Computer Board Research Project, begun in December 1986 with the aim of boosting Singapore's competitiveness in world markets. 50 companies participated in a pilot project launched in January 1988. This also included traders, customs agents and the Trade Development Board, which handles much of the documentation and licensing done in other countries by customs agencies. With Trade net, a trader's declaration is transmitted electronically to the Trade Development Board, which issues the necessary approvals within 15 minutes, after routing details to various government departments.

At times, depending on the types of goods, as many as 20 government agencies are involved. On receiving the approval, the trader prints and signs the document to obtain release of the cargo. This has made the life of traders quite comfortable for they have to no longer leave their offices to obtain customs approvals. They don't have to make special trips to rectify arrears or to resolve disputes. This has ultimately helped then in cost cutting. With storage of goods awaiting clearance no longer necessary, goods can now go straight from the ship to the consignee—a particularly important consideration in Singapore, where space is at a premium. This electronic clearance has made Singapore's port one of the most efficient in the world. The Singapore government has valued these efficiencies at more than one per cent of the GDP.

The financial system lies at the heart of a country's economy. The efficiencies or problems of the financial system travel to the rest of the sectors in a rather short span of time. It is the financial sector's efficiency that lies behind the success of developed economies. For instance, payments are transferred electronically between any two destinations in the 12 countries that make up the European Monetary Union (EMU), in less than five minutes. It would be nice if the same could be done between a business in Mumbai and its vendor in Delhi. Work that is held up for days for clearance of payments would then flow continuously. In this context, the dematerialisation of shares is also a revolution. It has done away with the hassles of handling paper and the anxiety of receiving share certificates in many months. This makes buying or selling faster and ensures better participation by common people, provided they make the right investment decision.

The world over and in most new private sector banks in India, long queues have given way to interactions with computer literate, efficient professionals. But the question is: Are we in a position to replicate this in all small and big financial outlets in India, say, over the next five years? However, since proven models are available in many countries today, it is really just a question of planning and doing it.

Regulating the Environment in a Transparent Manner

As mentioned in the beginning, the welfare government of a democratic country will do all that is in the best interests of people and therefore, wherever necessary, appropriate control or authority has to be exercised. It is not only enough that it be exercised, but that it should be done in a transparent manner that is appreciated by people. IT has played a crucial role in providing transparency.

Now government ministries and departments make available their reports and publications online. The union government's budget is available on the Internet minutes after its presentation. Progress of passport applications can be monitored online. Railway reservations can also be similarly made. After long years of information squeeze, people can now see and feel the functioning of the government machinery that is directed by their votes. As government functioning becomes more and more transparent, people develop greater confidence in its systems and processes. This will certainly add to the value of democracy. What does a transparent government mean to a common person? He wants his complaints to be heard and action taken. He needs basic amenities and opportunities. Not making information available easily raises suspicion. Transparency not only satisfies people, it also builds the government's credibility.

Dissemination of information and interaction with the public are key factors for quality governance. For example, the Securities Exchange Commission (SEC) of the USA, which is the equivalent of the Securities and Exchange Board of India (SEBI) makes it mandatory for companies incorporated in America to furnish their financial details to the SEC. This information is made public on its website. Furthermore, information can be demanded from the SEC and it publishes regular write-ups to caution foreign investors on their investments in the USA. The American financial system is perhaps the most transparent in the world. Anybody seeking any information either for his/her own use or for research can get it immediately. For example, an Indian researcher recently demanded from the SEC, details of a financial scandal that took place a decade ago. The SEC provided not only the documents pertaining to the case but also sent him similar cases to enable the researcher to take an informed view. Democratic nations need to set an example as far as transparency is concerned.

In India, some good models of various e-governance activities for development are now known to us. In Andhra Pradesh and Madhya Pradesh the connectivity and educational benefits of IT have penetrated to small villages. The Karnataka government has also become a successful player of the IT game.

STRATEGIES FOR REACHING OUT TO PEOPLE

Undeniably, in order to reach the masses and with a view to making them partners of the systems and processes of governance, greater emphasis needs to be laid on school education, especially computer education. The biggest challenge for this is making personal computers (PCs) available at an affordable cost. The Hardware Vision 2005 plan envisages PC penetration to 26 per 1000 people by 2005 from the present 6 per 1000. According to a Confederation of Indian Industry (CII) paper, the best way of achieving this would be to go local in terms of local needs, local problems, local solutions and local contents while making PCs affordable. Next to government and business establishments, schools would be the biggest consumers of PCs. The CII has estimated that 18 million PCs would be needed at the rate of 20 sets in each of the nine lakh schools in the country. To be affordable, the price needs to be brought down to below Rs. 15,000 per computer. This has implications for the tax structure. Custom levies are high in India in comparison to global standards. These are upto 35 per cent as compared to five per cent in China and Japan, two per cent in the USA, EU, Japan and South Korea to zero per cent in Singapore and Taiwan.

The Massachusetts Institute of Technology (MIT) and the Government of India have agreed to collaborate on a one-year exploratory project to create the Media Laboratory Asia, which is conceived as an independent, non-profit organisation. MIT plans to develop the technology to bring the benefits of the most sophisticated emerging technologies to the daily problems of India's poorest and least educated people. This would include assistance in formulating an innovative approach to research at the Media Lab Asia, providing guidance to identify potential funding partners and establishing working relationships between organisations in India and research groups at MIT.

The initiatives under the collaborative efforts of MIT and the Government of India to provide inexpensive computers with new ultra low-cost technologies from open source hardware to technologies for printing circuits, promises to dramatically bring down the cost of computing making locally produced computers widely available.

Television is today the best means of reaching out to the people, for 70 per cent of India views television. Popular programmes such as soap operas are considered effective means of reaching out to people. TV soap operas could explore new ways to educate, excite and enliven Indian communities on the role of technology in humanistic development.

The United Nations University, in Tokyo, dedicated to bringing peace and cooperation among the people of the world by increasing communication, has undertaken a massive programme of language networking so that language is not a communication barrier among the nations of the world. All organisational information of the United Nations is stored in a language independent form through UNL-ORG-Explorer. The key idea is to make it search and meaning based. This was finalised in a recent workshop in Geneva, organised by the United Nations University. Countries like France and Germany have shown keen interest and are providing heavy funding for the United Nations Language networking scheme.

The Media Lab-Asia in collaboration with IIT Mumbai has also undertaken an Agro Explorer programme so that farmers can benefit by various relevant information. The Ministry of Information Technology is very sensitive to the problem of language barrier and has therefore, introduced a scheme of technology development in Indian languages and IT localisation. Once the scheme becomes operational, it will go a long way in reaching out to and empowering the masses. This is an important strategy for the country's development.

CONCLUSION

The initiatives made by the Government of India and the Ministry of Information Technology, coupled with the success stories of Andhra Pradesh, Madhya Pradesh and Karnataka give hope that in the not too distant future, we will be able to achieve our target. The efforts of non-governmental organisations, educational institutions such as the IGNOU and the potential that lies in the collaboration between the Government of India and Media Lab Asia will show results in the next three to five years.

REFERENCES

1. *UNESCO, Working Document on Higher Education in the Twenty First Century—Vision and action*, Paris, 5–9, Oct., 1998.
2. *Knowledge for Development*, The World Development Report, 1998–1999.
3. *Entering the 21st Century*, World Development Report, 1999–2000.
4. *Information Technology Action Plan*, Government of India.
5. Fielden John, *Using Computers in Teaching and Learning: Strategies and lesson for managers*, London (unpublished).
6. Massachusetts Institute of Technology's Joint Project Document with Government of India on Explore Media Laboratory Asia, Released at the time of inauguration of the project in Mumbai, Government of India, July 2001.
7. *The Times of India*, July 15, 2001.

Bureaucracy: Changing Roles and Relationships A Transformative Agenda

— Dolly Mathew

INTRODUCTION

State, society and bureaucracy have assumed changed roles and responsibilities in the wake of liberalisation, privatisation and globalisation. The 'State' has evolved from an administrative to a cybernetic state. Civil society has developed into an institution influencing the state policy through public discourse and public dialogue. Bureaucracy now acts as an intermediary and a facilitator between the state and society. This has purported a change in its roles and responsibilities and also in its relationship with the state and society. Further, the changed role has also brought about a change in the internal structure and working of the bureaucracy.

THE CHANGED ROLE

Governance reforms aim at improving interorganisational governance structures, developing and improving process management and improving interorganisational decision-making. They draw theoretical inspiration from the theories on network management, negotiation and complex decision-making. Governance reforms like partnerships, interactive policy making and network management are aimed at dealing with the complex inter-dependencies between public and private actors. Eric Hans has treated partnership strategies as the rising of a network society. In such a society, public and private sectors are strongly intertwined. Government actors—public bureaucracies—function within networks of interdependent actors and thus help in the development of the society. The achievement of policy becomes a complex matter which needs cooperation from various actors. A hierarchical mechanism does not fit such situations very well. Hence, the need for transformation of the bureaucracy. There has been a powerful move towards increasing the efficiency of bureaucracy and also enabling private actors to deliver public services. This necessitates a change in the role of public bureaucracies in policy making and their relation with policy makers, and further suggests changes in their organisational structure and working culture, and their relation and interaction with the civil society.

In its new role, bureaucracy, has to incorporate openness in policy networks to enable partnerships. By adopting network strategies, it becomes possible to establish new ideas and transform inflexible thinking to facilitate the search for quality and to establish rules that facilitate partnering (Hans Eric).

Policy making, policy implementation, policy evaluation and assessing policy impact greatly depend on the effective cooperation of various societal actors and their contribution to it. Bureaucracies can establish fruitful partnerships among these actors, which have different perceptions, interests and goals and also coordinate their different activities so that actual results can be achieved.

With these changes, bureaucracy's relationship with the policy makers and the society, and its style of working also change. It is in this context that the changing role of bureaucracy can be explained.

BUREAUCRACY AND THE POLICY MAKERS

The relationship between the two is of complementarity. This means that elected officials and administrators need to help each other in a partnership for good governance. James H. Svara in his paper, *Myth of the Dichotomy: Complementarity of Politics and Administration in the Past and Future of Public Administration*, mentions that the complementarity of politics and administration is based on the premise that elected officials and administrators join together in the common pursuit of good governance. It stresses interdependence along with distinct roles; compliance along with independence; respect for political control along with a commitment to shape and implement policy in ways that promote the public interest; deference to elected incumbents along with adherence to the law and support for professional standards. Complementarity is basically the interdependence and reciprocal influence between the two. Svara contends that elected officials and administrators maintain distinct roles based on their unique perspectives and values and the differences in their formal positions, but the functions they perform necessarily overlap.

Jon Pierre finds the politico-administration relationship in today's world, a complex pattern of interaction and interdependence. He argues, it is a two-way phenomenon. On one hand, there is a 'politicisation of the bureaucracy': policy makers have increasingly come to realise that the bureaucracy is a source of tremendous executive powers and capabilities which require strong political control to ensure that they serve the objectives formulated by policy makers. On the other hand, there is 'bureaucratisation of politics', due to its higher degree of continuity and specialised expertise. The civil service becomes politically more assertive, more engaged in creating networks and linkages with other organisations and more inclined to use its discretion to pursue its own interests and ideals.

Thus, bureaucracy exists in a balance between political control and professional independence. Bureaucracy will work under political direction and equally adhere to professional standards in policy formulation and implementation. Respect for administrators by elected officials and commitment to accountability by administrators will add balance to the relationship. This will infuse flexibility in the working of the bureaucracy. Lessening of political control and providing political direction and tempo to civil services reforms will make the bureaucracy less susceptible to political pressures. This will lead to the redefinition and redesigning of bureaucratic procedures, tasks and operations which will help it to work better. These changes will also see the bureaucracy opening itself to the society.

BUREAUCRACY AND ITS ORGANISATION

Reforms in governance strive to alter the administrative behaviour, hence changing the bureaucratic organisational culture. Bureaucrats influence and are also influenced by the competing norms and values of the complex system of governance. They are squeezed between the demands of policy makers to increase efficiency on the one hand, and challenges from market based actors on the other. Together, these two forces induce bureaucracy to develop new routines, organisational concepts and skills for greater efficiency to compete with private actors in the sphere of service delivery. Bureaucracy has to be redesigned to be more accessible to the society and new measures of bureaucratic efficiency in terms of citizen satisfaction have to be introduced.

Democratising administration, managerial consciousness, reducing paperwork and secrecy, adopting new technologies, and training in ethics are becoming the features of bureaucratic re-engineering. There is a shift from cost, growth and control, to quality, innovation and service. The concepts of service, ethics, innovation, impartiality, fairness, participation and social engineering have become the new values for civil services. Changing the processes, combining several jobs into one, flatter rather than vertical structures, decentralisation instead of centralisation and job education in place of checks and controls are the current trends in bureaucratic style and functioning today.

The bureaucracy needs to be motivated to secure these changes The emerging New Public Service (NPS) movement, focuses on democratic citizenship, community and civil society. Organisational humanism and discourse theory require bureaucrats to exude a sense of strategic rationality (Denhardt). They are to acquire new skills of conciliation, mediation and conflict resolution.

Steps are to be taken to impart specialised skills training to bureaucrats. Also, providing them with detailed performance appraisals, a legal framework articulating their roles and relationship with politicians, right-sizing, eliminating redundancies, enhancing under-staffed departments and use of new technologies can increase their efficiency. Similarly, conducting recruitments and promotions to underscore merit and national diversity, prohibiting politically motivated transfers and dismissals and redressing the gender imbalance through affirmative action can improve the morale of the bureaucracy. Taking cognisance of values and beliefs, and changing them from protective to productive can reorient the bureaucratic culture. These changes will lessen political control over bureaucracy, bring flexibility in its working and enable it to open up to the society.

BUREAUCRACY AND CIVIL SOCIETY

Network management and interactive policy making are the trends in governance today. There is involvement of multiple societal actors like private, non-governmental, and voluntary organisations, individuals, the community, self-help groups, etc., in the formulation of policies. Bureaucracy has to bring these players to the table, facilitate and negotiate decisions and also create a sense of shared interests and responsibility. By supporting these groups and individuals, it builds a relationship of trust and collaboration with and among them. The relationship between bureaucracy and society depends on how the former is able to activate the different players, negotiate and help them achieve their goals through participation and collaboration.

Bureaucracy lays down the regulatory mechanisms for the private sector to ensure that the upkeep of social issues remains on the agenda of private sector functioning. It lays down policies for the empowerment of people, thus promoting consciousness and awareness among citizens and making the bureaucracy transparent, accountable and free from corruption. Today, the users of public services are also involved in service delivery. Jon Pierre, while highlighting the relationship between the bureaucracy and the society in different countries, found increasing cooperation between the two in the process of public service delivery, which helped in getting feedback from the people and ultimately led to improvement in the working of the bureaucracy. Denhardt and Denhardt opine that public officials will increasingly play more than a service delivery role. They will also have to play a conciliating, mediating or even an adjudicating role.

The accountability of bureaucracy is now multifaceted. It has to take into account constitutional law, community values, political norms, professional standards and citizen interests. Public servants have not only to facilitate solutions to public problems, but also have to be responsible for assuring those solutions are consistent with the public interest. Bureaucrats will work best when they are held in check by an active civil society. Citizens' right to appeal against public administration's decisions and rulings, their influence on policy and policy makers through various civil movements like the human rights movement and the feminist movement, their involvement in developmental activities through self-help groups like water user's association, *Mazdoor Kisan Shakti Sangathan*, etc., indicate the influence of the society on bureaucracy.

Therefore, bureaucrats have to be stewards of public resources, conservators of public organisations, facilitators of citizenship and democratic dialogue, catalysts for community engagement and at the same time street-level leaders (Denhardt and Denhardt). They can help in getting a deeper understanding of the state-society interaction and can operate as an interface between elected officials and civil society.

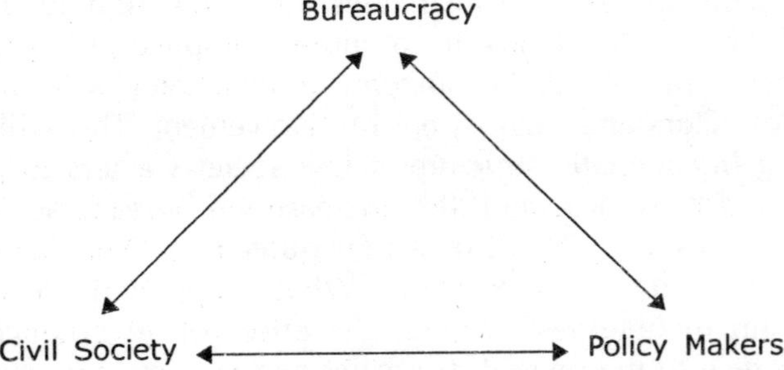

FIGURE 4.1 Interaction between Bureaucracy, Policy Makers and Civil Society.

The relationship of bureaucracy with policy makers determines the extent of flexibility in its working patterns. It further decides the relationship between bureaucracy and society. Lessening of political control enables bureaucracy to have flexible structures and thus, adapt to the changes in the environment and the society. Political leadership can make constitutional changes or reorganise the bureaucracy allowing it opportunities to take more initiatives, have greater discretion and be more accessible to society. The traditional style of bureaucratic functioning, with emphasis on security, order, rationality, legitimacy, anonymity, top-down approach and centralisation has been replaced with accountability, responsiveness, decentralisation, bottom-up approach, conflict management and transparency. This encourages the bureaucracy to strengthen individuals and groups in society, in building the community and involving it in policies and decisions affecting them. Public administration then operates as an interface between elected representatives and the society. Bureaucracy's flexibility allows it to penetrate society and also allows the society to influence policy makers through the bureaucracy. Likewise, enhanced public dialogue reinvigorates the public bureaucracy and restores a sense of legitimacy to it. With public dialogue and discourse, it becomes possible for people to influence the bureaucracy and policy makers to allocate the goods that are in the public interest.

CONCLUSION

Public bureaucracies were never constructed or designed to be efficient in the market sense of the term. The organisational design given to them was basically to make them amenable to the control of their political masters rather than to be of service to the people. Therefore, it is important to know the consequences of present day governance on public administrators. Today, the focus is on public service and building partnerships with the government, the community, the voluntary agencies and other societal actors in policy making.

Interactive policy making and network management generates tension with regard to the involvement of various actors in policy making. As the number of actors increase so also does the perception of problems and possible solutions. This leads to a more complex policy process and generates uncertainty about the outcome. Bureaucracy will have to decide the number of actors and their extent of involvement. This will decide how much existing bureaucratic structures allow societal actors to penetrate the bureaucracy and to what extent they increase the bureaucracy's capabilities to penetrate the society. Rajni Kothari (as quoted by Dipankar Gupta in his article 'Civil Society of The State: What Happened to Citizenship—Institutions and Inequalities') argues, the crises of governance is that the state is insensitive to the myriad diversities and culture of its people. Instead of responding to them, the state tries to stifle them in the name of political unity. The homogenisation efforts of the state negate the culture and talent of the people and foist a techno-managerial structure on them. The state prioritises the compulsions of a profit seeking market. How to reconcile the tensions between the state and society becomes a pertinent problem for the bureaucracy which has to toe the lines of its political mentor. Thus, there is need to understand the role of public administration for state—society interaction at large, and also to understand under what conditions public administration operates as an interface between elected officials and civil society and the consequences of this new emerging relationship.

With civil society actors getting involved in public service delivery, there has to be lessening of political control of the bureaucracy, thus providing it with more autonomy and flexibility so as to respond to the civil society and increase the number of contact points. However, giving too much autonomy may give too much power to public servants at the expense of elected officials, which may increase the risk of impropriety. There is need to strike a balance between the amount of autonomy given to bureaucracy and organisational efficiency, as more autonomy to bureaucracy causes significant problems in terms of control and accountability.

The new wave of good governance has brought in issues, which redefine the roles and relationship of the bureaucracy. This redefinition explains the changing nature of bureaucracy whose strength and importance lies in being dynamic. To quote Jon Pierre, "the only thing certain is that the public administration of the early 21st century will look different, behave differently and perform differently from those of the mid 20th century. Since the public bureaucracies of most countries have demonstrated considerable adaptive capacity during the 1980s and 1990s, we should expect them to be just as vital and dynamic in the future".

REFERENCES

1. Hans, Eric. K. and Geert R. Teisman, 'Managing public private partnerships: Influencing processes and institutional context of public private partnerships', *Governance in Modern Society*, (Ed.) Oscar Van Heffen, Kluwer Academic Publishers, Netherlands, 2000.
2. Denhardt, B. and J. Denhardt, 'The new public service: Serving rather than steering', *Public Administration Review*, Vol. 60, Nov.–Dec. 2000.
3. Haque, S., 'The diminishing publicness of public service under the current mode of governance', *Public Administration Review*, Vol. 61, Jan.–Feb. 2001.
4. Heffen, O.V. and P. Klok, 'Institutionalism: State models and policy processes, Governance in Modern Society', (Ed.) Oscar Van Heffen, Kluwer Academic Publishers, Netherlands, 2000.
5. Bruijn, H. and E.T. Heuvelhof, 'Process management', *Governance in Modern Society*, (Ed.) Oscar Van Heffen, Kluwer Academic Publishers, Netherlands, 2000.
6. Pierre, Jon, 'Comparative public administration: The state of the art', *.Bureaucracy in the Modern State: An Introduction to Comparative Public Administration*, Edwar Elgar, 1999.
7. *Human Development Report in South Asia*, The crisis of governance, human development centre, OUP, 1999, Karachi, Pakistan.
8. Esselbrugge, M., 'Interactive policy making as a serious alternative balancing between an open and closed approach', *Governance in Modern Society*, (Ed.) Oscar Van Heffen, Kluwer Academic Publishers, Netherlands, 2000.
9. Riccucci, Norma M., 'The 'old' public management versus the 'new' public management: Where does Public Administration fit in?' *Public Administration Review*, Vol. 61, March–April 2001.

Responsive Administration of the Criminal Justice System in India

— K.K. Sharma

INTRODUCTION

Good governance has been an eternal challenge to rulers since the emergence of the state, irrespective of its nature, structure and form. It is a dynamic concept. In the contemporary world, good governance is associated with efficient and effective administration in a democratic framework. Simply put, good governance envisages a responsive administration that is citizen-friendly.

We have taken impressive strides in various fields, viz. economic development, arts, science and technology. However, our politico-administrative functioning leaves much to be desired. The government is struggling to perform its primary functions such as maintenance of law and order, security of the state—internal and external, prevention and investigation of crime, and prosecution and rehabilitation of criminals.

An effective criminal justice system is an essential component of good governance. According to the National Police Commission, 'the fundamental basis for any criminal justice system is the law of the land, especially in a democratic society. The very process of evolution of law in a democratic society ensures a measure of public sanction for the law through consent expressed by their elected representatives. The entire criminal justice system in our country, therefore, revolves around laws passed by the Union Parliament and State Legislatures'. The durability and credibility of the system will, in the first place, depend on the inherent strengths and weaknesses of the various laws enacted from time to time. After laws are made in the legislative bodies, their enforcement is taken up by various agencies set up by the government.

The criminal justice system covers the entire scenario from the occurrence of crimes, investigation, adjudication proceedings, correctional services and finally the administration of jails. Police, prosecutors, advocates, judges and functionaries in the correctional services and jails form the different, distinct organised wings of this system.

The ultimate objective of the system is to secure peace and order in society. The success of the system, therefore, depends largely on a proper understanding of the objectives of the system by all the wings and their coordinated functioning to secure this objective. Thus, the criminal justice system consists of four parts, namely:

1. The making of laws.
2. The enforcement of laws by the police.
3. Trials by judicial courts.
4. Jail and other aspects of correction.

The current crisis of governance in India can largely be traced to the failure of the criminal justice system to perform its due role. In the ensuing paragraphs we will be discussing the aforementioned aspects in detail.

THE MAKING OF LAWS

The government began to think of the problem as early as 1955, the Law Commission was appointed to revise and modernise the judicial system. But in the last 47 years, the number of pending cases has increased to the extent where thousands of cases have had to be withdrawn. Thousands of men and women languish in jails as undertrails for long periods. The number of laws have multiplied while procedures have become more and more complex. One can justifiably conclude that justice is perishing in our land. Instead of making justice cheap, effective and substantial, we have done the opposite. While we have tried to make small amendments, all our basic laws bear the imprint of the times in which they were made. A lot of them may be relevant, but many need to be updated.

It seems to be a practice developing all over the world to make a brief law, with proper delegation of legislative power to the executive minister to make the rules and to be responsible for implementation. This has the obvious advantage of reducing the load on the legislative machine. Now the tendency is to include all details in the law itself; to tell the bureaucrats not only what work should be done, but also who should do it, how it should be done, how to guard against mistakes, and even how to take action against departmental shortcomings and watch the result.

In order to deal with all aspects of the criminal justice system as one, the Law Commission's terms of reference should be expanded to deal with law, police, courts and jails. The commission already deals with two aspects—law and courts. Jails and police can also be taken up with the help of a special committee or commission. A continuous study of the problems of criminal justice seems essential by a statutory body, which has competent technical backing, and the ability to stimulate public thinking and debate. In this process, help for studies and data should be taken from police research institutions like the Bureau of Police Research and Development and Institute of Criminology and Forensic Science, the training academies of the civil and central services, law colleges, sociologists, retired judges, administrators and politicians.

A vital need for India is a parliamentary committee to review the implementation of laws. If the committee could have at its disposal a large databank, it may be able to keep track of all problems connected with law-making and national development.

ENFORCEMENT OF LAWS

The police and administrative machinery of the state are expected to enforce the laws as per laid down procedures. The law requires them to act independently, fearlessly, impartially and decisively with courage and passion. There is lack of close cooperation between the investigation and prosecution agencies. This hampers the putting up of cases in the court. Close cooperation between the two is therefore necessary. After carefully examining the various aspects of reorganisation of the prosecution agency, the Administrative Reforms Commission recommended, 'while the prosecuting agencies may be functionally separate from the investigating agency as at present, a common measure of coordination at the district level by the Superintendent of Police may be ensured'.

The National Police Commission also corroborates this view. According to the commission the first task in modernising the police should be to make sure that they are never allowed to use illegal or improper methods. Secondly, a good officer should be given security of tenure and support to do his job firmly. Thirdly, we should weed out from the police, undisciplined men.

Modernising the police will probably be more difficult and certainly more expensive than the other two operative parts of the criminal justice system—courts and jails. Since Independence, we have allowed the machine to fall into such a bad state of misuse and disrepair that a thorough overhaul is absolutely necessary. And before we think of any other reform, we have to ensure that the machine is used in the right manner for the prevention of crime.

The National Police Commission has made some important recommendations, which are mentioned as follows:

1. It is imperative that we modernise the police in every way with our ingenuity and within our resources.
2. There is a need to set up a State Security Commission in each state consisting of members both from the government and the opposition, and citizens, to monitor performance and to suggest policy changes to the government. The Chief Minister or the

Home Minister can be the chairman of the commission. The main object should be to insulate police from politics.

3. An immediate judicial inquiry should be made mandatory in cases of rape, death or hurt being caused in police custody and when two or more persons die as a result of police firing.
4. Grievance redressal machinery should be set up on the model of the staff councils.
5. The Law Commission should be expanded into a Statutory Criminal Justice Commission with representatives from all sections of the criminal justice system. It should analyse crime causation, demographic, social, economic and psychological causes; devise laws, and help the police to find suitable solutions.

TRIALS BY JUDICIAL COURTS

Laws declared by the Supreme Court are binding on all courts in India. All civil and judicial authorities are to act in the aid of the Supreme Court. The Supreme Court and the High Courts have been declared courts of record and have the power to punish those who commit contempt of court.

The following are defects in the system of criminal trials:

1. A large majority of those committing serious crimes are not apprehended and prosecuted.
2. Those charged with minor offences, and unable to get bail, have to wait as undertrials for years and years.
3. At least 75 per cent of the cases prosecuted could be disposed of by the magistrate at the first hearing, if he is so empowered.
4. Those who are guilty of serious crimes are not punished promptly because of endless procedural delays, which make it very difficult to get a conviction.
5. The law does not give adequate protection to the weak and the underprivileged.
6. Legal aid is unknown in most states.

Court trials and disposal of cases can take anything from five to twenty five years with a pendency of over 2.5 crore cases all over the country. By the time cases are tried, some witnesses may be won over or be dead, or be disinterested in the case to the point of genuinely having forgotten it.

While the Constitution endeavours to provide equality to all citizens, the entire societal structure is based on inequality. A poor man cannot afford the best legal talent to get justice. Even if no new cases are instituted, it will take at least ten years to clear the backlog. Courts are overcrowded and overworked.

We also have to tackle the procedural lacunae by identifying the causes of delay and devise every possible method of expediting quick and clear decisions. We have to introduce summary trials, mobile, honorary, and village courts. Part-time tribunals to try divorce, dowry, motor vehicles, landlord-tenant disputes and related cases should be set up. Paying specified fines by post, summons by post, limiting session's trials to 30 days, introducing photo copies of documents, restricting rights to appeal—for instance, by the government against High Court decisions, can expedite the disposal of legal cases. The police should be given greater power for direct disposal of cases so that the workload on the courts may be reduced.

JAIL AND OTHER ASPECTS OF CORRECTION

Our jails are terribly overcrowded. The real intention of imprisonment is to rehabilitate the criminal. But, the general manner in which the rituals of daily life are rigidly administered and enforced inside jails, tend to dehumanise the prisoner. Jails do not function to reform and rehabilitate the criminal.

Some correctional measures need to be taken to reform the jails. Justice Krishna Iyer has suggested the following:

1. The attempt of the whole system should be to keep as many people out of jail. Some unorthodox measures, other than imprisonment, such as probation, warnings, deferred sentence, personal bond, employment in a project or factory, or as a cook in a hotel can be used.
2. Open prisons, low security prisons for *satyagrahis*, work of some type for undertrials and payment for that work must be introduced.
3. The procedure of release from jail should be easier and specialised, and not based on someone's personal judgement that a convict has not been punished enough.
4. Parole and non-institutional programs should be designed to keep convicts in touch with the outside world as well as to build up an easy return to normal life. Medicare should be developed.
5. Each jail inmate must have the benefit of proper legal advice.

CONCLUSION

There is no denying that a criminal justice system is one of the basic prerequisites of good governance. Making of laws, maintenance of law and order, public order, internal and external security of the state, protection of human rights, administration of justice, and reformation of convicts are the primary duties and responsibilities of government. No government can hope to survive if it fails to perform these functions. The image of the criminal justice system determines to a large extent the image of a government. Thus, an efficient, effective, and responsive criminal justice system is necessary to ensure good governance.

REFERENCES

1. *Administration Reforms Commission*, 'Report of the Working Group on Police Administration', 1967, p. 58.
2. Asmerom, H.K., K. Borgman and R. Hoppe, 'Good governance, decentralisation and democratisation in post-colonial state', *Indian Journal of Public Administration*, Vol. 41, No. 4, Oct.–Dec. 1995, p. 736. Also See, Special Number on 'Towards good governance', *Indian Journal of Public Administration*, Vol. XLIV, No. 3, July–Sept., 1998.
3. Bata, K. Dey, 'Defining good governance', *Special Number on Towards Good Governance*, op. cit., pp. 413–415.
4. *Crime in India*, National Crime Records Bureau, Ministry of Home Affairs, 1996.
5. Mishra, B.N., *Juvenile Delinquency and Justice System*, Ashish Publication, New Delhi, 1991.
6. Bayley, David H., *The Police and Political Development in India*, Princeton University Press, Princeton, New Jersey, 1969.
7. For details, see, *Law Commission of India, 114th, 116th, 117th, 120th, 121st Reports* on Gram Nyaylaya, National Judicial Services, Training of Judicial officers, Manpower planning in judiciary and a new Forum for Judicial Appointments, respectively.
8. Mander, Harsh, *The Sunday Tribune*, April 14, 2002, p. 12.
9. Roy, Jaytilak Guha, *Policing in Twenty-first Century*, Indian Institute of Public Administration, New Delhi, 1999.
10. Julio, Ribeiro, *Bullet For Bullet*, Viking, New Delhi, 1998.
11. Sharma, K.K., *Law and Order Administration*, National Book Organisation, New Delhi, 1985, p. 129.
12. Gajendragadkar, P.B., *Law, Liberty and Social Justice*, Asia Publishing House, Bombay, 1965.
13. Bhakshi, P.M., *Decriminalization: A Study*, Indian Law Institute, New Delhi, 1994.
14. Mukherjee, Satyanshu K., *Administration of Juvenile Correctional Institutions*, Sterling Publisher, New Delhi, 1974.
15. Section 162 of the *Code of Criminal Procedure* and Sections 25, 26, and 27 of the *Evidence Act*.
16. Nath, Trilok, *The Indian Police: A case for a new image*, Sterling Publishers, New Delhi, 1978.

6

E-governance: Options and Opportunities

— P.K. Mehrotra
— Alok Ranjan

INTRODUCTION

Today, governments the world over are faced with the challenge of meeting the growing requirements of people. There is increasing concern about their administrative capacity and organisational efficiency to give the best to their citizens. In response to this challenge, most governments have administrative reforms programmes. These administrative reform programmes primarily focus on the following:

1. Improvement in service delivery to people.
2. Empowerment of people through dissemination of information.
3. Increasing transparency in government business and government transactions and reducing corruption.
4. Establishing synergy between the public and private sectors.
5. Achieving system efficiency through the promotion of knowledge networks.

Information Technology (IT) helps in reinvigorating government by enhancing the ·administrative capacity and organisational efficiency. Application of IT leads to the following:

1. Increased transparency in administrative processes, thereby reinforcing people's faith in the government.
2. Opportunities for promoting participation of people and their organisations in government processes.
3. Openness in the functioning of the government.
4. Innovations and introduction of new ideas and concepts in government transactions.

5. Evolution of intuitive solutions to development issues and problems facing the community.

E-government is the name given to IT driven public and development administrative system, which essentially means delivery of government services and information to people using electronic means. E-government also implies the ability of people at large to obtain government services through electronic means, enabling access to government information and completion of government transactions on an anywhere-anytime basis.

E-government has a number of advantages over the traditional system of government. Some of these advantages are as follows:

1. Lower costs and improved efficiency and quality of government services.
2. Effective linkages between the government and the citizens.
3. Improved efficiency of the government.
4. Increased transparency and accountability in government business.

This chapter presents the different contexts in which IT has been applied to public administration throughout the world. It discusses the key issues related to the universalisation of the use of IT in public administration. The chapter also highlights the limitations of Information Technology and the e-government model in improving efficiency and effectiveness of public administration. It also highlights the options available for promoting the application of IT in the government.

INFORMATION TECHNOLOGY IN GOVERNMENT

Information Technology is the electronic means of capturing, processing, storing and communicating information. It is based on the concept of digitisation of information. Digitisation converts information of any form and nature into digital form, in which all information is held as 1 and 0. It is basically a combination of computer hardware and software and communication networks, the most popular of which are telecommunication networks. Developments in the field of computers and innovations in telecommunications have made Information Technology user-friendly and cost-effective.

Information Technology has the potential of improving people's access to government information and use of information pertaining to development and welfare activities. It provides the cheapest, quickest and easiest way of accessing government information.

Information Technology facilitates the acquisition and absorption of knowledge, offering the government unprecedented opportunities to enhance educational systems, improve policy formulation and execution, and widen the range of opportunities for business and the poor. It has the potential of enhancing system capacity, improving the processes of policy formulation and execution, widening opportunities and institutionalising innovations.

IT has been found to facilitate informed decision-making in public administration thereby improving its efficiency and effectiveness in delivering services to people. It enhances the analytical capacity of public administrators, thereby promoting comprehensive monitoring and assessment of the performance of development and welfare activities and their impact on the life of people. Information Technology has also been found to facilitate innovative use of information collected and maintained by the government in the form of imaginative information linkages and information sharing at all levels of the government. IT is particularly helpful in establishing a two-way information communication network, vertically as well as horizontally across the organisation.

Government sponsors a number of independent studies and evaluations about the performance of the government and efficiency of public services. Such studies generate a lot of information. However, a very small proportion of this huge and varied information available with the government is currently utilised in the policy formulation and decision-making processes within the government and also in planning for development and welfare activities. It has been repeatedly stressed and argued that a more effective and efficient use of the information available with the government can lead to significant improvement in the administrative capacity and organisational efficiency; and can promote informed decision-making. Information Technology has the potential of increasing the utilisation of information in government transactions, in planning, implementation and evaluation of development and welfare activities as well as in assessing the impact of the welfare and development activities on the life of the people. The user-friendly features of IT ensure that it can be used even by persons who have limited technical expertise. Application of Information Technology in government, therefore, provides an opportunity and scope for reinvention of the government.

MODELS FOR E-GOVERNANCE

The models for e-governance can be grouped into the following four broad categories:

1. The General Information Dissemination Model
2. The Critical Information Dissemination Model
3. The Advocacy Model
4. The Interactive Model

These models are now discussed at some length.

The General Information Dissemination Model

This category of e-governance model is the first, but most crucial model for the application of IT in government businesses and transactions. It is also regarded as the first step in the transition from traditional government to e-government. It is limited to the dissemination of government information, already in public domain, to a wider public domain through the application of IT. This is usually done by publishing government information on the Internet.

The General Information Dissemination Model is based on the assumption that informing people about the functioning of the government helps in establishing a better rapport between the people and the government. Informing people also empowers them to exercise their rights and responsibilities and make informed decisions. This model also remedies a situation of information failure. It is an essential prerequisite for creating an environment for enhanced participation of people and their organisations in government businesses and transactions.

The following are some examples of the General Information Dissemination Model:

(a) Publishing government laws, regulations and legislations on the Internet so that they are available at anyplace and at anytime to people.
(b) Making available names, addresses and contact details of government officials on the Internet.
(c) Publishing information related to various welfare and development schemes and activities on the Internet along with the details of procedures for availing benefits of these schemes and activities.
(d) Publishing information about the performance of the government on the Internet.

The Critical Information Dissemination Model

This model differs from the General Information Dissemination Model in the sense that it is restricted to the dissemination of critical information to a targeted audience or in a wider public domain. The application of this model requires an understanding of the 'use value' of the information set that is being made available. It also requires the identification of potential users of the critical information. Unlike the General Information Dissemination Model, this is an action-oriented model. By providing a critical set of information, this model promotes information based decision-making and action either by a specific group of population or by people at large. It becomes possible to know the lacunae in the government, take cognisance of people's interests and opinions in the decision-making process. It fosters public debate, opinion and censures on all issues related to the development and welfare of the people.

The Critical Information Dissemination Model can be applied in the government in the following ways:

(a) Publishing corruption related information on the Internet.
(b) Publishing research studies, enquiry reports, impact and evaluation studies on the Internet.

(c) Publishing on the Internet reports on human rights violations by the government and its agencies.
(d) Publishing information related to the environment and climate on the Internet so that it can be used by farmers and citizens.

The Advocacy Model

This model can be viewed as an aid to civil society to influence the, government decision-making process by forming virtual communities or specific groups within, as well as outside the government. It enables public debate on issues related to public welfare. The model can help the government by directing strategic flow of information to groups of communities who can become strong virtual allies to complement government action. It mobilises the potential of human resources and information, overcoming geographical, institutional and bureaucratic barriers and targets them for concerted action on pertinent issues facing the community.

Formation of virtual communities helps them to share similar values and concerns, promotes active sharing of information among them and links them with real activities for concerted action. The Advocacy Model enhances the scope and participation of individuals and communities in open debates and discussions on governance, welfare and development related issues. This creates an effective deterrent for the government and other decision-making agencies and makes them watchful of their actions.

The Advocacy Model has been applied to the following areas of governance:

(a) Fostering public debate and discussions on issues of larger concerns.
(b) Building pressure groups in the society to pursue specific causes.
(c) Publishing the opinion and views of the oppressed and deprived sections of the community on the Internet so that these can be incorporated in government businesses and transactions.
(d) Catalysing wider participation of people in the government's decision-making processes.
(e) Building global expertise for decision-making in situations where local capacity and expertise for information based decision-making is lacking.

The Interactive Service Model

The Interactive Service Model is a consolidation of the three models of e-governance described earlier. It opens up possibilities for participation of people in government businesses and transactions. Unlike the first three models of e-governance, which are basically one-way information flow models, this is a two-way information flow model, in which the potential of

Information Technology is fully utilised. Because of its interactive nature of operation, this model leads to greater participation, efficiency and transparency. It also results in substantial savings of time and cost in the decision-making process within the government.

The Interactive Service Model ensures direct connectivity and linkages of people with government representatives and officials. As a result, the government's functioning changes from representative-based to individual-based, and from a passive, reactive nature of actions to a pro-active one. Thus, this model helps people in having greater access to and control over the administration. This access and control, in turn, makes the public and development administration system more responsible and accountable to people's needs and expectations.

The Interactive Service Model is now used universally in the delivery of public services to people in developed countries. In developing countries like India, the application of this model is limited. Because of its interactive nature, it is very technology laden and cost-intensive. Another factor that limits the application of this model is people's lack of elemental familiarity with Information Technology. Such an elemental familiarity is currently missing in India because IT penetration among the masses still remains superficial. In such a situation, putting the model in place may not be of much benefit as the majority of people do not have the capacity and skills to use the services available to them.

The following are the areas of application of the Interactive Service Model:

(a) Election of government officials and representatives.
(b) Grievance redressal, feedback and reporting system.
(c) Sharing of concerns and common interests by people and the government.
(d) Organisation of opinion polls on government policies and other government decisions.
(e) Decentralised forms of governance.
(f) Online government operations.
(g) Interactive channel of communication between key policy makers and members of the Planning Commission, etc.

CRITICAL ELEMENTS IN E-GOVERNANCE

There are four critical elements of e-governance—information, technology, processes and people. These four elements constitute what is known as the Information System.

However, e-governance, cannot operate in an institutional vacuum. It can succeed only in an enabling institutional environment and a set of influencing factors that may be political, legal, economic and even social and cultural. Putting all this together, the basic frame work for e-governance has been shown in Figure 6.1. We will first deal with the Information System and then with the environment.

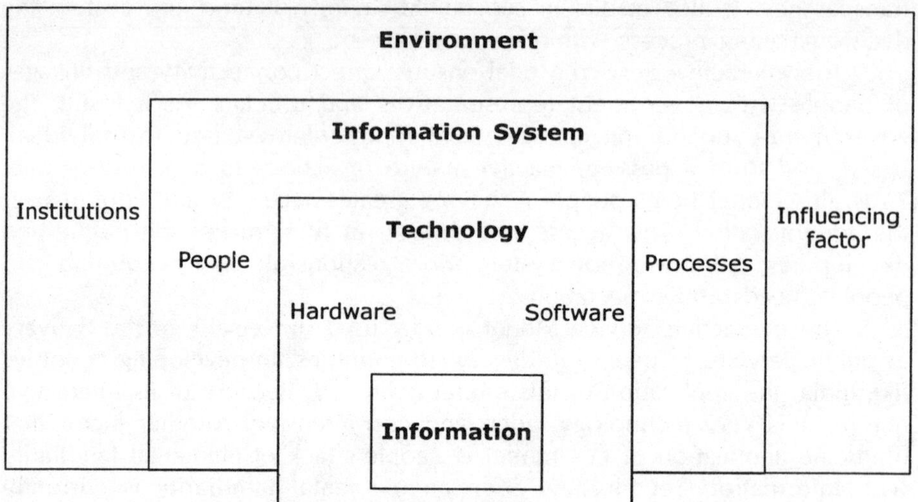

FIGURE 6.1 A Systematic View of the E-governance Model.

Information System

The Information System consists of information and technology to put the information to meaningful use, the processes which use information for any purposeful activity and the people who are capable of using the information through the application of technology to defined processes. All the four elements—information, technology, processes and people—of information system are critical to e-governance. If any of the four components of the system is found to be missing, e-governance cannot work.

Information

Information is the core of the e-governance model. Availability of information is the first and most crucial requirement for the implementation of the model. A well-defined and well-organized system of information collection, storage and retrieval and a well-established system of updating available information at regular intervals is critical to the success of the e-governance model. It is also important that the system of collection of information is such that the whole process is transparent and the information collected is of a high quality, so that people can have faith in the available information. Moreover, information that is most suited to the application of the e-governance model is the information that is related to the people and not to the government itself. E-governance can succeed only when it is built upon information that is related to those to whom it is directed to serve—the people and their groups.

Another important issue is the accessibility of the information available with the government by the people at large. There are three views.

The first is that the information available with the government should be made freely available. This view argues that people have the right to see and use the information which, with certain exceptions, relates to them.

The second view contends that government information is owned by the concerned government department or agency, which invests in the collection and storage of the information that is of substantial commercial value. As such, government information should not be made freely available. Rather, it should be made available for a certain price. People may obtain government information and use it as long as they are able to pay for the required information.

Finally, the third view about the available information with the government, does not see the information as important enough to warrant open consideration of issues of ownership, value and charging. Information is virtually regarded as a personal asset of a particular department or agency. The information is generally not made available and people do not have rights of access.

E-governance conforms with the first view of making information available and accessible to the people.

Technology

The second requirement for e-governance is the availability of information in electronic format. This raises the issue of hardware and software necessary to transform the information available in the paper format to electronic format.

One technical issue in the application of the e-governance model is the interlinking of information available at different levels and across different departments and agencies of the government. Networking of all sources of information, vertically as well as horizontally, becomes very important for the success of e-governance.

A complete discussion on the technology needs of e-governance is beyond the scope of this chapter. However, two points are of relevance here. First is the cost consideration. The cost of hardware, software and networking required for universalising the use of Information Technology in government may be a deterring factor in pursuing e-governance in a poor country like India, where electronic technology is viewed more as a luxury than a necessity for administration. Moreover, Information Technology is changing so rapidly that standardising the technology for e-governance is extremely problematic. It may be stressed that standardizing the technology is essential for its wide use at all levels of administration.

The second issue is that of the digital divide across which one group of population reaps the benefits of Information Technology while other group cannot. Computer literacy or elemental familiarity with IT is essential. Not everyone has these skills and so they remain cut off from computers and the Internet. Governments are generally well aware of the limitations of Information Technology leading to *social exclusion* that prevents a group of people from fulfilling their economic and social potential. Attempts are being made to enable people at large to avail the benefits of IT. However, Information Technology based inequalities are expected to persist in the coming years. In such a situation, replacing paper-based and face-to-face availability of government information by electronic information may not help to promote e-governance. A more modest approach may be that of supplementing paper-based information with electronic information. It will lead to substantial increase in the cost. What is even more important is the fact that all the effort may address the technology barriers but not the skill barriers. To a majority of the people, skill barriers mean they require the assistance of an intermediary or facilitator who will train them to or help them in gaining access to and using the electronically available information.

Processes

The third important issue in e-governance is redefining and redesigning the government processes. The current system of governance has evolved over the years in the context of paper-based information and not in the context of electronic information. In order to promote e-governance, provision of Information Technology based processes in the government needs to be laid down. In the absence of such a provision, paper-based information and paper-oriented government transactions will continue to be preferred over electronic information.

Paper-based government cannot be replaced by new Information Technology processes in one go. This can happen only gradually. Moreover, new processes can replace traditional ones only when the technology and human skills required for adopting the new processes are in place.

People

The last component of the Information System necessary for e-governance is the human resources with necessary skills to use the IT. The availability of skilled manpower is perhaps the most formidable challenge in the promotion of e-governance. There are two reasons for this. Firstly, most governments, today, are involved in reducing the workforce and so there is little scope for recruiting new and completely skilled staff. Secondly, the existing government workforce is not properly oriented towards Information Technology. There have been attempts to train the existing workforce in the basics of IT, but the experience has not been very encouraging.

The Environment

Another requirement for promoting e-governance is an enabling environment that helps in institutionalising the concepts and processes of the e-governance model in the government as well as in the society. Both, the environment within the government and the environment outside the government are important for promoting e-governance.

The first and foremost requirement for building an enabling environment for e-governance is policy initiative. The e-governance policy must clearly identify the limitations of e-governance in government. Application of Information Technology has its own limitations, which must be highlighted in any policy initiative.

The next important step in creating an enabling environment for an IT based government relates to developing frameworks and institutions rooted in Information Technology. This may require a comprehensive restructuring and reorganisation of the existing bureaucratic system and administrative hierarchy.

A third requirement is the enactment of necessary rules and regulations. This may require amendments in government business rules. Legal sanctity to IT based processes and transactions is critical for maintaining the credibility of the e-governance model in the eyes of the people. A legal framework for the application of the e-governance model is also necessary for information security and for dealing with cyber crimes in an effective manner.

CONCLUSION

E-governance is a step towards reform in government and administration. These reforms focus on bringing improvements in the service delivery, dissemination of information, transparency, public and private partnership, efficiency and accountability. The various models for e-governance that is, the General Information Dissemination Model, Critical Information Dissemination Model, Advocacy Model and Interactive Model, aim at providing information to a wider public domain through the application of IT. These models help in publishing government laws, regulations and legislations, making available the names, addresses and contact details of government officials, highlighting the performance of the government; and furnishing corruption related information, research studies, enquiry reports, human rights violations and environmental information on the Internet. These models foster public debate and discussions, elicit opinions and views, catalyse wider participation and organise opinion polls. They help in facilitating reforms in governance.

The four elements of the Information System—information, technology, processes and people—enable e-governance to function. Likewise, e-governance also requires an institutional environment with a set of influencing factors to operate. E-governance thus entails the options and opportunities for providing services to people in a more efficient and effective manner.

Achieving Excellence Through E-governance

— **J.C. Kapoor**

INTRODUCTION

The need for good governance for a country's development cannot be overemphasised. The challenge before the government, at this juncture, is greater than ever before. The turbulent business environment that is prevailing in the world in general, and in India in particular, has triggered a compelling need to search for a new management paradigm that will enable the government to succeed. There is an urgent need for the government to get closer to its citizens. While quality of service is a prerequisite, innovation and speed would add value. There is a need to draw up a clear strategy to redesign governmental processes and to recognise and select good technology solutions to give good governance. E-governance will offer a new vision to governance, and an opportunity to obliterate age-old systems that have now turned anachronistic.

E-GOVERNANCE IS GOOD GOVERNANCE

E-governance is good governance and every government is supposed to provide good governance to its citizens. However, in the context of e-governance, there has to be adequate emphasis on 'governance'. Governance needs to be 'e-enabled'. E-governance is concerned with the relationship between citizens and government. The role and processes of governance need to be redefined and redesigned with reference to citizens' needs and aspirations. Citizens want excellence in governance—high quality of governmental services delivered on time and at minimum costs. They want governance to be citizen-centric. The focus must change from 'procedure-orientation' to 'service-orientation', from 'supply-driven' to 'demand-driven' governance.

The renewed debate on the problems of governance and administration, and emphasis on new public management seem to have been born out of the frustration of the common man for not receiving the quality of service that he expects or pays for. The efficacy of the governmental way of managing the affairs has been questioned and debated time and again. Can governance be improved? Does e-governance offer new opportunities to help achieve the kind of governance we ought to have? What style of working do we need to adopt to increase our capacity to meet our objectives? Can we change our mindsets to build a 'vision' for excellence in governance for the future? Is it time to bring response systems and organisational processes and structures in tune with the changes in technology? Can Information and Communication Technology (ICT) empower the common citizens of the country to get their due?

NEW VISION FOR GOVERNANCE

There is a need to change the mindset. Nothing short of a total overhaul will do if governance is to succeed in a difficult environment. There is need to draw up a clear strategy to use wisdom and knowledge for recognising and selecting good technology solutions. The present chaos in governance presents a real opportunity. This is an opportunity to architect a completely new vision for governance, an opportunity to obliterate age-old systems that have turned anachronistic in the new global scenario, and an opportunity to make innovation the 'life infusing force' to revitalise governmental organisations and make them organic, in the true sense of the term. The intention here is not to argue how it can be done. The methodology and the technologies of e-governance are available, all of which are application-neutral. And that is the strength of e-governance.

E-GOVERNANCE IS CITIZEN-CENTRIC

The objective of citizen-centric governance is to ensure that the interests of citizens are safeguarded. This will need a complete reorientation of citizen-government relationships. It will necessitate a complete redesign of governmental processes. This has to be much more than a website or a new delivery window. It should ensure simple and trouble-free service to the citizens. Thus, e-governance should facilitate the lives of citizens.

In fact, a major part of corruption in public life would be eliminated if personal contact between the citizens and the government officials is reduced. With e-governance in place, the moment a citizen goes online to a 'governance portal' using his or her identification and password, referred to as 'digital certification', he or she can automatically get access to any of the services, irrespective of their physical location. The citizens will be able to know online their liabilities to any government department, file any return, pay any bill or tax without actually going to a cash counter. They will be able to file their application for renewal of driving license or ration card online. A large number of citizens continue to be critical of the urban authorities for wrong billing and long queues for payment of water, power, and telephone bills. This can be lessened with the computerisation of citizen services.

SOCIAL SECURITY AND E-GOVERNANCE

Most developed countries of the world spend a significant part of their GDP on social security schemes for their citizens. The benefits offered are in the form of unemployment doles, health cover, old-age pension and maintenance allowance for children of separated couples. Their e-governance systems are in place for online submission of personal particulars, identification, verification, evaluation and authorisation of benefits under various social security schemes. In India, there have been attempts by state governments to offer social security benefits to citizens. There is a need to design and issue a Citizen-I Card to every citizen. It should be possible to use the same card for voting, getting a driving license, availing government assistance, welfare programmes and subsidised food through PDS. It should be a 'smart card', readable conveniently, anytime, anywhere, through a hand-held card reader with a policeman, at a ration shop, at a kiosk located anywhere, including remote rural areas, or at home. It does not matter what Indian language the cardholder reads or speaks, the kiosk or computer will respond in the language of the cardholder. With the IT Act in place and the Controller of Certifying Authorities having been appointed, it is possible to authenticate or certify digital signatures. To prevent frauds and for greater security, it is possible to have biometric images captured on the smart card. Logging on to any e-governance portal through such a card is highly secure and any transaction can be made through this mode.

E-GOVERNANCE APPLICATION AREAS

Education

The development of a country is dependent directly on the status of education in that country. While at one end of the spectrum is the country's dismal performance to promote literacy, on the other, there is continuous addition to the number of educated, unemployed youth in the country.

Government efforts to remove illiteracy have not led to satisfactory results. E-governance can be used to overcome this problem. Mass literacy programmes through the Internet, at the *panchayat bhavan* of a village, in the form of interactive sessions filled with games, fun and stories can be designed and implemented. Information on need and availability of education, irrespective of the government (central, state, or local), department, or section should be available online and the aspirant should be able to avail of the desired services online.

Rural Services

One of the most innovative ventures in rural development has been the *Gyandoot* programme in Madhya Pradesh. It is a community-owned, self-sustainable, low-cost intranet model implemented in Dhar district. Computers placed in the *gram panchayat* buildings have been connected through an intranet and are managed by the local rural youth, generally matriculates. They work as entrepreneurs without any salary or stipend. The software is menu-driven and highly user-friendly. The operators need the bare minimum skills to operate the kiosk. The services available to users at nominal prices include: online registration facility, copies of land records, agriculture produce auction centre rates, government programmes, etc. An interesting educational service available for school children is online career counselling.

Information about the eligibility for loans, prices of fertilisers and seeds, prices of agriculture produce, availability of diesel, the power-cut schedule, agricultural implements, spares for tractors and other equipment can be made available on the Web. Likewise, copies of land records, application to the government and facilities for payment of electricity bill can be made available through the Internet. One can imagine the cost, time, and effort involved in doing all this by physically going to government offices. If governance is about providing services to rural areas, it has to be e-enabled. The solution lies in empowering the rural masses with the information they need and at the time they need it. The information and services they need must be provided online and at their doorstep.

Industrial Labour

There is an immediate need to establish e-governance for the three major social security functions of the Ministry of Labour of the Government of India. These are: Employees State Insurance (ESI), Employees Provident Fund (EPF) and employment exchanges. Employees Provident Fund Organisation (EPFO) has 23 million members and the Employees State Insurance Corporation (ESIC) provides social security protection to 35 million industrial workers. Employees of the organised and unorganised sectors, small, medium, and large factories, establishments, and organisations and their families are directly affected by these functions, which are instantly amenable to e-governance. This would ensure a high level of satisfaction to a large section of the society and mobilise and save huge financial resources of the concerned organisations.

The financial figures of arrears to be recovered on account of non-compliance or under-payment in the EPFO are mind-boggling. ESIC gives medical care and cash benefits to insured workers through more than 1400 dispensaries, 140 hospitals, and its regional and sub-regional offices spread all over the country. The service delivery system is weak in the sense that settlement of claims is a very cumbersome and slow process, and workers have to travel long distances to personally visit the ESIC offices for small and trivial matters. There is no properly compiled database of insured persons. There is no unique identification of the insured person and his family members. Consequently, it is not possible to verify the person's identity and authorise him for receiving benefits. Many insured persons have been found to possess more than one benefit card with different names. The loss on account of pilferage of benefits is enormous. Also, in the absence of instant reconciliation and online transmission of funds to the ESIC account, there is a huge loss of interest on the pipeline money.

The e-governance solution to the three functions is to enable all users to communicate with the system online for all services they are entitled to. Knowing the status of the account, updation in the PF account, filing of insurance claim under ESI and submitting online employment applications would save the beneficiaries from the inconvenience of long waits and travel to get the benefits due to them.

Issue of Passport

In spite of the fact that the Regional Passport Office in Delhi and its branches have their own websites that give the status of an application for issue of an Indian passport, it takes about three months to issue a passport. However, if one has the right connection or contact with an agent, he may get it faster. The governmental process is linear in nature. The application must go from one stage to another to reach its final destination for a final decision. Can some of the activities be performed simultaneously? Can we cut on time? E-governance may have the solution. It would enable an applicant to submit his application (including photographs and signatures) online to the regional passport office. The application would automatically and simultaneously go to the special branch in the police headquarters, the concerned district police, the police station and all other offices concerned with the issue of passport. All clearances and objections by the concerned offices can be filed online. In this way it should be possible to issue a passport within a few days to all eligible applicants. This would also eliminate any personal contact between the officials (passport and police) and the applicants. With the IT Act and the Controller of Certifying Authorities in place, transmission of any content, including photographs and signatures should be no problem.

Issue of Driving Licence and Registration of Vehicles

Issue and renewal of driving licence has been streamlined to some extent by the transport authority in Delhi. Unfortunately, governance has not been able to get rid of touts, medical practitioners issuing medical certificates and studios issuing quick photographs in the licencing office. The reason is simple. The process demands personal contact between the applicant and the officials. Online submission of applications would eliminate long queues in the office, and dispatch of the licence through mail would eliminate all personal contact between the officials and the applicants. There is enough scope for implementation of e-governance for online registration of vehicles. Registration of new vehicles and allotment of registration numbers by the dealer/supplier to new vehicles is a good step in this direction. However, a lot more can be done, particularly, in the matter of transfer of old vehicles. A large number of vehicles change hands every day. Many of them are not transferred in the name of new owners. Some vehicles end up in the hands of anti-social elements. While permitting transmission of information by the old owner about the sale of his vehicle to a new owner, great care has to be taken to ensure the identification of the original owner. The e-enabled process can help the police to watch out for vehicles being transferred frequently.

Payment of Taxes, Bills, and Submission of Returns

It should be possible for a citizen to pay taxes and duties of all kinds online. Filing of income tax returns, sales tax, house tax, etc., need to be facilitated through the use of ICT. This would reduce, if not eliminate, the need for personal contact with the concerned government official and the consequential manipulation. The problem with the existing governance processes is that the citizens are supposed to do a lot of running around to various government offices to get clearances and submit information and documents to all the offices. They have to deal with the whims and fancies of officials in these offices. With e-governance, it is possible for various departments to come together to serve the needs of individual citizens. The prerequisite would be that each department has its own interactive and up-to-date website. An individual citizen can log on to any of the sites to get a service from any of the departments. While any individual government department would offer, by itself, the services available at that particular site, it may provide a linkage to all other departments or related departments for services offered by those departments. However, the website of the Government of India (GOI) should provide linkages and access to all departments all over the country. A citizen should be able to log on to the GOI site for any department like education and social welfare, sports, income tax, environment, commerce, health, etc and then interact with the concerned department. He can also log on to the GOI site to access any of the services like payment of property tax, sales tax, income tax, issue of birth or death certificate, ration card, or payment of electricity, water, or telephone bills, or filing of any return or complaint.

E-policing

A common citizen feels harassed if required to visit a police station to lodge a complaint or a (First Information Report) FIR against any violation of law. Things would be different if such complaints can be filed online through e-policing. The acknowledgement and action taken can also be communicated online. Traffic violations and the alleged attendant corruption/payoffs represent some of the most glaring examples of bad governance. A hand-held electronic card reader-cum-recorder, with electronic speed sensors will help in punishing traffic offenders. Electronic synchronisation of traffic signals on main roads will be a boon for road users. Tamper proof electronic fare metres installed on taxis and autos would save the citizens from harassment at the hands of the unscrupulous operators of these services.

Customs Clearance

The customs and excise department of the Government of India has introduced the concept of electronic data interchange in respect of imports and exports of air cargo. The concept, though limited in scope so far, has to be enlarged to ensure huge savings in cargo clearing cost and time, loading and unloading of ships, and storage and handling of containers at the container freight stations in the country. The largest economic activity of the country—imports and exports—involves five entities: ports (or airports), shipping lines (or airlines), customs, container stations and importers (and exporters), in the process. Though the customs work at the port is computerised, there are long queues for entry of shipping bills into the computer before an exporter gets permission to cart the cargo into the container station. Once in, similar details are entered in the computer at the container freight station. An integrated e-governance solution would ensure that the exporters transmit their shipping bills electronically from their offices before their containers leave their factories. The computers at both, the customs and the container station, would thus, automatically get all the details before the container arrives. When the cargo arrives, the terminal operator at the gate enters only the container number to verify the details and grant permission to cart the cargo into the container station. This process would take a few seconds as compared to several minutes (at times an hour or so) taken at present. But then, there would be no direct contact between the exporter and the concerned staff. In this manner, the efficiency would, perhaps, increase manifold.

Controlling Encroachment of Public Land and Unauthorised Construction

The problems of encroachment of public land and unauthorised construction in a city like Delhi have reached menacing proportions. The government procedure and the lack of initiatives make it almost impossible to take any action against the defaulters. E-governance may offer some possible solutions provided there is a will. The reality is that a common citizen is afraid of complaining against any influential person, particularly, when the identity of the complainant may get revealed. While e-governance offers transparency and can make all information available online, it can also block any information from any user. Honest citizens will not hesitate to participate in the government's effort to solve the problem. A fully e-enabled system can be developed and implemented to monitor the status of every single property in the city. Complete mapping can be integrated into an online database for the purpose. It can also be linked to the water supply, electricity connection and property tax systems.

CONCLUSION

The government, today, has to focus on providing efficient and effective services to its people. Due to greater awareness, people now play an important role in the service delivery of goods. E-governance makes this possible through the use and application of Information and Communication Technology in rendering services to the people. Internet based kiosks, community centres, computerised facilitation counters are the means to provide quick and efficient services to the people. The need is to provide good governance with dwindling resources. Government must find a new way to work—it must re-engineer for results, and redesign its processes. It has to examine its mission and look into the question as to how, on a day-to-day basis, it can deliver. It has to fundamentally change its way of doing business so that it is responsive and accountable to the citizens who are the key stakeholders in the developmental process. It has to create computerised facilitation counters available online to eliminate the endless maze citizens have to negotiate in order to obtain services. It has to change its structure, service delivery and technology base to strengthen quality through vital performance measures. There has to be a culture committed to quality, excellence and continuous improvement in governmental working.

8

Information Technology and Governance

— Sanjay Jaju

INTRODUCTION

Effective use of Information Technology (IT) is increasingly becoming synonymous with good governance. Still, the government appears to be apprehensive about switching over to IT solutions to solve the problems of governance. Why is technology an anathema to governments? Why are governments so averse to change? Why is there no public pressure on the so-called responsible governments to use the technology and change? How have governments immunised themselves against such pressures, if and when they are applied? Will the fate of governments be forever hinged on their efforts and success in meeting the challenges posed by external events? The answers to these questions are the essential pre-requisites for us to figure out the shape and nature of governmental response to the needs of Information Technology.

Information and Communication Technology (ICT) is transforming the way life goes on, but to date, this change has been limited to a range of activities in certain technology-intensive enterprises. Other sectors, including the not-for-profit and public sectors, have lagged behind. The pace of change and the opportunities and risks, which are being presented, are of such potential significance that efforts need to be made to ensure as broad a base of participation as possible.

Information Technology is all about connectivity. Connectivity brings proximity, which improves the delivery of services by the government. Local self-governments deserve maximum attention as they are at the cutting-edge and therefore immensely affect the daily lives of the citizens. It is in this context that a project called Saukaryam (meaning facility) was launched by the Visakhapatnam Municipal Corporation for delivering a host

host of civic services online. The project was completed as a public-private partnership initiative at no additional costs for the corporation within two months of its conception and commissioning.

THE WAY AHEAD

As a first step, let us put across certain basic facts—known and unknown—about governments in general. Governments are the principal users and disseminators of information and the general perception is that they are not able to do a good job of it. Just as the survival of any business depends upon the material and mental satisfaction of its customers, the survival of governments is also hinged on the contentment of its citizens. The exploration of this interface, the areas where government and citizens meet, is vital to our understanding of where and how technology should intervene to make this interface more transparent and less of a botheration for both partners. Besides this, the relationship between various partners within the government also needs to be included in this arrangement so that the benefits of technology can accrue to them as well. It is also essential to sensitise the citizens to the post-technology use scenario so that they are well prepared for the required task. Against this backdrop, let us look at the status of the interface between the government and the citizens.

Presently, the relationship is more of a benefactor-beneficiary kind. Citizens have become used to waiting in long queues, getting insensitive and harsh interim responses, greasing the palms of officials for making anything move or getting it stalled. Citizens don't complain as they think that it is of no avail. They feel helpless and unmotivated. The rot has entered the psyche of the citizens whose reaction is either silent submission or overt connivance with such practices.

How can IT help mitigate this? The extreme reaction to this may be de-governmentalisation. A less extreme reaction is to improve this relationship wherever and however possible. Information Technology surely can play a part in the latter and help us better our lives.

Information is the government's biggest equity and it is essential that it be used for greater public good. Quick access to information is possible by making it available in the public domain. Once governments decide to do this, market forces would ensure that private operators get into the act. They would start filling in the infrastructural and other gaps at no costs to the government. It would now be worthwhile to discuss the areas where IT can make a material difference to the quality and speed of service delivery.

Access to Public Documents

Various government orders, schemes, programmes, annual budgets, gazette notifications, legislation like ordinances and bills, and examination results fall under the category of public documents. This category covers all those areas where the citizens need quick and accurate information from the government, but presently get it with great difficulty or at private costs. This will also ensure citizens get information without exorbitant communication costs.

Authentication of Statements

This includes the areas where citizens need certificates from competent authorities in the government, such as copies of land records, registration of sale and property deeds, birth/death certificates, and various other permissions required under various acts of the central, state and local self-governments. The principle here is that the process of sorting, calculating and reading through a huge database is best done by a machine and should be done so.

Online Payments

Payment of taxes, duties, rents and rates, including the payment of user charges for facilities offered by government departments, payment of electricity, telephone and water charges, and road and irrigation cess would come under this category.

Filing of Statutory Returns

Citizens are required to file returns under various statutes of the central and state governments ranging from the obligations under excise, customs, income and sales tax acts to declarations and affidavits in the courts. Online submission should make life easier for both the parties.

Complaints, Grievances and Suggestions

Filing, redressal and follow-up of complaints pertaining to the facilities offered by the government is possible through IT. There may be an online forum both for the government to get the feedback on its policies, pronouncements and actions and for the citizens to ventilate their feelings and air their differences.

Partnering with the Government

Such areas where the government does business with the private sector like outsourcing work contracts, leasing out services or making purchases could benefit from IT interventions. An online and transparent government would instill confidence resulting in improved communication.

Online Delivery of Services

Connectivity and digitisation in areas like health care, education, policing, and civic amenities like fire services, rescue, relief and rehabilitation operations during calamities should make their delivery better and more cost-effective.

Within the Government

The gains of technology can be applied equally to improve the systems within the government. The various departments and wings of the government depend on and feed into each other. The time and energy taken to process and send information to various sections within a department and to various departments severely impede the decision-making process and becomes a breeding ground for corruption.

There is an endless list of areas where technology can make governments do a better job. In fact, it is difficult to list any function of a government, which can't be improved by using technology. The good news is that most governments have woken up to this fact. Let us hope this is not too little and too late.

An example of how Information Technology could impinge upon human lives and can help governments perform better is the Saukaryam project which was conceived, developed and implemented in Visakhapatnam Municipal Corporation. The project provides a host of civic services by using Information and Communication Technology.

VISAKHAPATNAM MUNICIPAL CORPORATION'S ONLINE CIVIC SERVICES PROJECT: SAUKARYAM

People well-governed should seek no other liberty, for there is no greater liberty than a good government. This becomes pertinent and has far-reaching implications in today's context when the waves of change point towards a liberal economic framework and the exit of the state from sectors that could provide better services through private enterprise. While this is so, it definitely does not mean curtains for governments. As long as civilisations last, governance in some form has to exist to ensure order and fair play. Its areas of operation may change, but societal dependence on the state is inevitable. In that case, it is important that the state does its task in a manner that provides least inconvenience and maximum facility to its citizens. Never before has there been such a strong craving for looking at the options and alternatives to improve governance. Though there are many ways of achieving that, one has to find methods that are easy and cost-effective. It is here that the tools of Information Technology score over others.

Before starting Saukaryam, the following fundamental principles were kept in mind:

1. Information Technology rests on connectivity. A stand-alone computer could offer only minimal utility, and therefore, networking would be essential to maximise the gains. As interactions become digital, they could be coordinated over greater distances, creating new communities of interest and new challenges for governance. While talking of networking, speed and security would be the prime considerations.
2. Computerisation should not be an end in itself, it should only be the means to achieve a larger goal. This goal would maximise citizens' satisfaction about the delivery of civic services. The system would therefore keep citizens at the centre and every process would be designed keeping this in view. This meant that back-end computerisation would not be attempted unless it had a public outreach. Attempts to improve internal efficiency would also be directed at citizens.
3. The design of the system would be Web-enabled as the Web offers the easiest method for citizens to gain access to the information they need. The website, instead of carrying reams of static information, would be utility driven and carry dynamic linkages to the office intranet. This would also help citizens avail a host of civic services online without leaving the comforts of their homes.
4. The project would be designed as a public-private partnership model that would involve cost and revenue sharing with the private sector. Such a model, being self-sustaining, leads to more accountability due to multiple stakeholders. In any case, cash-starved governments have no other alternative.
5. The biggest challenge for any computerisation exercise is to ensure a meeting of the minds of the system designer who may be from outside the organisation, and the system developer who is part of the organisation. The system developer knows the nitty-gritty of the system much better but lacks skills. Therefore, insiders possessing computer skills need to be involved to develop a model for a computerised system improvement plan in a much better manner.

Based on the aforementioned fundamental principles, Visakhapatnam Municipal Corporation went about the task of onlining all its civic services.

Online Payment of Municipal Dues

All governments depend on the taxes and revenues they raise from their citizens. The government's financial management hinges on a sound, transparent, efficient and foolproof tax collection system and the ease and flexibility with which the citizens are able to pay their dues. Before the project was put into place, the citizens were required to go to the ward office and get in touch with the tax collector for calculating and preparing the payment *challans*. As the entire operation was manual, searching through the records and carrying out the required calculations would invariably take time. In the event of the absence of the tax collector, the citizens had no option but to waste their precious time and energy. The citizens also did not have any idea about the calculations the corporation had made while determining their dues. This led to resentment as it made citizens visit various municipal corporation offices for such calculations. The system also led to a lot of paperwork at all levels entailing huge costs and time delays. The reconciliation of the amount collected by the banks and its remittance to the municipal account was also a time consuming job.

The Municipal Corporation of Visakhapatnam is now using Information Technology to improve the system. The corporation has computerised all assessments. All the records are maintained in a server available in the municipal corporation's office. The server has been connected through a local area network (LAN) with computer nodes available in the local bank branches. Only those local bank branches have been selected, which have voluntarily come forward to provide the necessary hardware and agreed to make use of the facility. A private partner has connected these nodes to the main server through a broadband network running in the city. The assessees now carry this demand notice to any of the earmarked bank branches where, after entering the assessment number, they instantly get complete information with updated calculation of the demand and arrears alongwith the interest, if any. Once the citizen pays the amount, the bank just updates the records on the main server at the click of a mouse. The bank is able to acknowledge the payment through a printout issued to the citizen on the spot. All partners benefit. Banks get ready cash, the networker gets business, while the citizens can make their payments in ease.

The system also enables the corporation to get the ward-wise, demand collection statements which helps in easy monitoring of cases with huge pendencies and prevents delinquents from escaping the tax net. As the system also provides for automatic posting of penal interests for delayed payments, the discretion of tax collectors in waiving such amounts gets eliminated. The system has also led to improvement in the efficiency of tax collection. This is corroborated by figures. For instance, this year the corporation could collect 50 per cent over and above last year's collections with the same staff and similar costs.

The updated information is also listed on the corporation's website. Citizens can get updated information about their property taxes by entering their assessment number.

Security

One important consideration in the digital maintenance of any network database is protection and security. Every user sharing this database through the intranet is given a secret password without which access to the database is denied. Such access is also limited to the requirements of the individual user. Day-to-day transactions are encrypted and posted in a separate database. The existing information is then available for comparison with the encrypted information for detecting and avoiding any tampering, hacking or misuse. The possibilities of introducing firewalls and other security measures are also being explored and implemented.

A UTILITY DRIVEN WEBSITE: www.saukaryam.org

The World Wide Web or the Internet provides the most cost-effective method of reaching out to the people. The Web can not only help in the speedy dissemination of information but can also help the citizens to access various services, which hitherto required their physical presence. In order to realise this objective, the corporation's website was launched under Saukaryam. The evolution, development and maintenance of the website is done on a public-private partnership platform, so as to infuse more energy, better ideas and ensure that it remains vibrant. While developing the website, it was made very clear that it was not to be merely an information driven website. It would be a utility driven website that would enable outsiders to gain access to the corporation's intranet and local area network. While the static page information has been hosted on a foreign server, the dynamic pages are hosted on the corporation's server and are also accessed through it. In this manner, the necessity of continuously updating and uploading information, which is the bane of most websites, has been avoided. All the dynamic pages get their inputs regularly as part of the in-house computerised network and get updated in the process.

Now, at the click of a mouse, citizens are able to see their property dues any given moment or can access the required birth and death records. They can also look up the infrastructural works being taken up by the corporation, while contractors can access the various tender notices issued. A builder can check the status of a building application made by him, while citizens are able to track the status of complaints or grievances made by them through the Internet, through the civic centre or in person. Besides these utilities, the website also gives the citizens information relevant to their city, like weather, news, places to visit, and train and bus timings.

The citizens have a right to know about the functioning of the government machinery as it is directly related to them. However, as the activities of the enterprise increase, so do the formats, rules, bylaws, procedures and orders that govern them. The website also gives information related to the calculation of property tax, related procedures and building rules and regulations. In addition to this, it provides entrepreneurs with information on business possibilities and opportunities available in the town. The website also carries linkages to the office intranet to allow the management to gain access to it from anywhere by using their passwords. By acting as a window to the corporation, the web site is drawing huge attention and has had more than 40,000 visitors. It also offers space for further incorporation of new avenues.

CITY CIVIC CENTRE—THE ONE STOP CIVIC SHOP

Not everybody in a country like ours has an access to the Internet. People do not even possess the basic knowledge of computers. To mitigate this, a computerised City Civic Centre has been established under the project. This allows the citizens to access civic services. The centre has a string of computers on the network and allows citizens to avail facilities like getting birth and death certificates, filling water tap/drainage connection requests, applying for building plan approvals, lodging complaints/grievances, making miscellaneous payments, etc. In fact, everything that required physical presence can now be transacted on the Internet.

As the Civic Centre is on the network and is connected to the main server, which in turn is connected to the global Internet protocol, citizens can track the status of their application through the corporation's website. For doing so, a unique registration number which can be used to track the status is alloted to every applicant. The system also helps system managers and the corporation management to carry out internal monitoring of the disposal and redressal of such applications to eliminate any chance of delay and harassment leading to nepotism and corruption. The operations of the City Civic Centre have also been connected to the Web thereby bringing in transparency about the number of applications received and the concerned department to which they relate.

The popularity of the Civic Centre can be gauged by the response that it has got from the citizens. It is frequented by not less than 200 persons everyday seeking various services. As broadband network is used for local area networking, the geographical expansion and spread by opening more such centres for meeting future needs would not be very difficult.

Online Filing and Settlement of Complaints and Grievances

The Municipal Corporation's website provides citizens the facility to lodge complaints and grievances online. The grievances get forwarded to the concerned officer for necessary action and also go into the database for monitoring grievance settlement. The key point to note here is that all the complaints and grievances, which the corporation receives, either through the Internet or through the Civic Centre or in person, go into a common database and are therefore available for rigorous monitoring. The module also provides for forwarding and transfer of complaints from one officer to another in lesser time than it would have taken normally.

One can also find out the number of grievances pending with various officers at a given instance. This is proving to be very useful for monitoring the efficiency of various sections. The status of the complaint and its disposal gets instantly communicated to the complainant, so that he or she can see the action being taken and give the necessary feedback. Although disposal of complaints has to be done at the field level, the project provides a mechanism to monitor such disposals in order to prevent hardships to the people. As the whole module is linked through the Internet, it is possible for any officer to monitor the complaints received by him from anywhere. It allows all the officers the facility to issue virtual instructions for taking immediate remedial actions.

Online Tracking of Building Plan Status

The Municipal Corporation engages in the task of approving building plans, subdividing plots and regularising structures within the city limits. The citizens have no clue as to the status of respective cases. The website has opened the floodgates of information to the public through the Internet. Now, at the click of a mouse, the status of the application is known without running from pillar to post. The entire process of scrutinising, processing and sanctioning of building plan approvals has been computerised. This allows online tracking and monitoring of the movement of any such paper within the town planning section. This has also helped the section in meeting the statutory deadlines set for the release of plans and also allows citizens access to the status of disposal of their applications. The project also envisages the creation of a building plan database and its subsequent hosting on the site so that citizens are able to know the exact nature of the approval given and are not lured into buying unapproved buildings creating future complications for themselves.

Online Registration of Births and Deaths

Every citizen is a valuable human resource for the country. Registration of births and deaths is therefore mandatory. It becomes everybody's responsibility. The corporation website provides to all, the list of hospitals registered with it, the facility to send birth and death information online, after charging minimal incremental costs. Previously, the entire operation of collecting information from the hospitals and maintaining it in the master records used to take years. It became primarily the responsibility of the citizens to ensure that the concerned sanitary inspector sent the required data to the Corporation. Even after collecting the information, the whole database, which used to be maintained manually was the preserve of a few corporation officers, who would take a lot of time to search for the required records. Now, the information from the registrar instantly comes through the virtual mode without any mediation.

Instant Issuance of Birth and Death Certificates

Citizens are able to get their certificates delivered to them quickly.

Maintaining a computerised database of births and deaths has simplified the process of sorting, searching and accessing the information. Citizens are also able to get their records updated as they have the facility of checking whether their name is registered or not through the website. As the certificate has to be issued in the physical world, the City Civic Centre provides citizens the facility to instantly collect their certificates on demand as the records pertaining to them have been thrown open. Citizens can now get necessary rectifications made in their records without any delay.

Online Tracking of Garbage Lifting

The Municipal Corporation also enters the daily lives of the citizens in many ways. On the one hand, it has to keep the city clean and sanitised, while on the other, it has to cater to the water requirements of the city. The Corporation also arranges for street lighting, roads and basic infrastructure. Citizens are now able to know how all this is being done and by whom. At the click of a mouse, they can see the sanitation plan of their street or the water supply plan of their ward.

The process of lifting garbage from the city and taking it to landfills was previously not documented and only manually accounted for. This practice led to corruption, inefficiency and ineffectiveness. Now, the collection of garbage at the landfill and its weighing has been computerised and the same data has been uploaded on the website. It is therefore possible now for the citizens to check the status of garbage removal from their wards at any specific date. The system has also helped the Corporation to internally streamline its operations and fix responsibility for poor sanitation.

Infrastructural Works Online

The process of sanctioning infrastructural works and their processing within the organisation has been computerised. This has helped the Corporation to monitor and track the execution of such works. It also helps in preventing expenditure beyond the sanctioned budget. The entire module has also been linked to the website so that citizens are able to see the infrastructural works being taken up in their respective ward areas and also monitor their status. This has especially helped the political representatives and media persons who used to previously run around for getting this basic information. This has brought in transparency in the execution of works, as details furnished online clearly indicate the name of the contractor, the amount sanctioned and the current status of the works. It has also helped the contractors to look at the tender notices online thereby making the whole process more open, transparent and accountable.

Online Citizen Forum for Furthering Democracy

The website also provides a virtual meeting place for citizens to discuss civic issues, problems and prospective solutions. Citizens now freely interact with each other and post their ideas on the website which acts as an online forum for citizens to ventilate grievances, air opinions and cause necessary social change. The website also provides online facility to philanthropists and citizens who wish to contribute funds for their city and make an impression for themselves. It also lists projects and business ideas. It inspires citizens to adopt parks, traffic islands, participate in community development and other activities for the betterment of their city.

The Corporation office is full of visitors seeking personal attention. Now, the website provides citizen's the opportunity to chat online with the mayor and the commissioner and tell them about their problems, offer suggestions and ideas, give feedback and remind them about the work not done. This is only a beginning as the areas where technology can make governments do a better job are endless. The gains are palpable. Citizens are getting used to the site, considering the response it is getting. The spread of Internet kiosks is a harbinger of community coming together.

FREQUENTLY ASKED QUESTIONS ABOUT THE PROJECT

What Does the Project and the Website Entail?

Saukaryam is a project for the online delivery of civic services and is a vibrant example of how community informatics can improve the lives of citizens. It is a first of its kind project built on a public-private partnership platform and improves the delivery of municipal services through Information Technology. On the one hand, the project uses the Internet while on the other, it provides a local broad base through call centres connected through a broadband network spanning over the city to cover an area of over 120 square kilometres. The guiding principle while developing the project has been complete internal computerisation and networking. At the same time intranet application in a user-friendly format has been put on the Internet for public use.

The project provides the whole gamut of civic services ranging from the payment of dues to lodging of grievances to filing building plan applications and getting their status online without running from pillar to post. There is also a facility for hospitals to send birth and death information online, helping citizens get their certificates quickly. As the Municipal Corporation affects the daily lives of citizens in many ways, all such areas have been covered. Now at the click of a mouse, citizens can see the sanitation and water supply plan and also get updated information on the infrastructure works being executed in their city. It also provides contractors online tender notices and entrepreneurs and philanthropists the business opportunities and social possibilities. It has also provided an online forum for citizens to ventilate their grievances, air their opinions and cause necessary social change. In short, every service offered by the city corporation is extended online under this project.

Why is the Project Unique?

The project is the first of its kind in the country and provides most of the civic services in a user-friendly format by using Information and Communications Technology. The project recognises that information is the government's biggest equity and it is important that it uses it for greater public good. The project has helped the civic body throw open relevant information to the public. The utility driven website developed for the project is unique and serves every need of the citizens who used to previously face a great deal of harassment at the hands of the corrupt and insensitive bureaucracy. The project has brought in transparency, accountability and speedy delivery of services. It has helped reduce unnecessary visits to government offices. In a developing country like India, where the dependence of people on the government is very high, the project has helped better people's lives immensely. One important feature of the city website is its dynamic nature and the fact that it is based on an office system that is fully computerised and therefore updated instantaneously and automatically. Another first is that being multi-disciplinary in nature, it covers all aspects of governance ranging from taxation to public works to city sanitation. It has acted as a tool for uniting communities, which is important for a diverse nation like India.

How Does it Use Information Technology for User Interaction?

This is an Information Technology based project and user interaction is through call centres on the one hand and the Web on the other. The project, for example, gives citizens the facility to pay their municipal dues. This they do by going to select centres established in local bank branches connected to the main server through a broadband network. The local branches use the software to gain access to the main server. This software has been developed in-house and is secured through passwords and encryption technology. The users also interact with the Corporation through the Web site, which comprehensively covers all civic areas. They have the facility to file grievances online. These get directly forwarded to the concerned officer, thereby reducing the time taken to handle a grievance.

The system has also brought in transparency and accountability to administration by loading relevant and hitherto inaccessible information on the Web. The citizens can, at the press of a button, see the daily efficiency of the sanitation staff in clearing garbage or see how the infrastructure projects are being executed. Under the project, the entire system of work sanctions has been computerised. Putting information on the Internet has enabled contractors and the public to have access to it, thereby improving the accountability. The website is an outlet for citizens to access the office intranet which encompasses all sectors and therefore makes available the latest information without requiring any conscious efforts to update the portals.

THE RESULTS OF THE PROJECT

The results have been stupendous. Ever since the project was commissioned, it has become the talk of the town. Citizens are surprised and enthused by the ease with which their needs are getting attended to without their running from pillar to post like before. The harassment they used to face, for something as basic as paying their dues, at the hands of insensitive and corrupt bureaucrats has been eliminated after the advent of this project. This is clearly established by the jump in Corporation revenue after the current system was put into place. Complaints like abrupt drinking water supply or non-functional streetlights that earlier took months to enter the system now get attended to in no time. This can be gauged by the number of hits that the site is attracting everyday and also by the increasing number of registered users.

The project has been covered in the national and provincial media and has been hailed as a model to be replicated elsewhere. The citizens forum has become a virtual meeting place for citizens to freely air their views on the city's development. This opportunity was earlier the prerogative of only a few leaders in a representative democracy. Many call centres catering to the project are coming up in areas inhabited by weaker sections. This reflects its popularity across the whole range of communities. The computerised, swanky and prompt reception-cum-information centre that the project has helped in developing is in stark contrast to the dusty, crappy, citizen-filled manual centre that existed previously.

THE MAJOR BARRIERS TO ITS DEVELOPMENT

Resistance to change is inevitable, especially if the status quo gives vested interests additional clout. This project also met with a similar response as the bureaucracy reluctant to open up created many hurdles to see that the power it wielded over the information in its control was not reduced by bringing it into the public domain through the Internet. It was only after sustained pressure and coercion that the bureaucracy yielded the desired information. Besides this, the openness and transparency in administration, which the project attempted to achieve was also feared by those sections of employees who did not want to get exposed for their inefficiency. Another constraint was the paucity of funds as is case with most of public bodies in

India. This was why the project was taken up as a public-private initiative with entrepreneurs investing in it. The effort involved in laying the broadband line through the length and breath of the city was a herculean task especially when it was to be done in a short time. Another challenge was to develop public awareness about IT and get the citizens to use the medium created by the project for accessing civic services. The political acceptability of the project was another challenge that was successfully met when the chief minister of the state decided to replicate it elsewhere across the state.

PLANS FOR THE FUTURE

Saukaryam has already become a pilot project for municipal governments and is being replicated in other parts of the state. Which is why, it is important that all the loose ends both on the software and the hardware front, are tied up. Though sustainable in its present form, the project may need additional resources for upscaling. Arrangements to tie up additional resources, especially from the private entrepreneurs would be firmed up. The project has a potential for becoming a government portal and other areas of governance are proposed to be built on the project. As the project evolves, more features will be added to make it more user-friendly. By itself, informatics cannot surpass social, political and economic barriers to development and good governance but it is a *sina qua non* for any social project that attempts to do so. The widening knowledge and information divide can increase the already existing class gap in this country. The project could play a major role in reducing this.

THE KEY TO SUCCESS OF THE PROJECT

Saukaryam is an example of how big tasks can be easily done, if broken down into small 'doable' tasks and assigned to various stakeholders at the right time. The project involved many distinct areas ranging from data collection and computerisation, to networking and establishment of call centres as outlets for citizens to access the services offered by the project. The services were broken into manageable tasks and outsourced to entrepreneurs ready to work as partners in the project. While the data was entered and updated by the Corporation staff software and programme development was taken up as a joint exercise by the in-house software wing and private site developers willing to have stakes in the project.

All across the city, networking was done by a private bandwidth supplier in lieu of which he was offered rights to run the line for other commercial applications in the city. Most of the call centres were opened in the local bank branches that invested in the provision of necessary hardware in lieu of which they were allowed to retain the collected funds which gave them liquidity advantage for a fixed period. By roping in many stakeholders, the project could be completed in three months from the time of its conception without any additional burden on the already stretched financial resources of the Corporation. There is a big lesson to be learnt from this. Anything is possible provided there is a will and the partners are persuaded to tag along by giving them stakes in a public non-commercial activity.

THE EVOLUTION OF THE PROJECT

The project came about when the author, as Commissioner, went for a round of the city and found a group of people gathered in an office, waiting for the local tax collector to come and write demand notes for them to pay their taxes. To enquiries about how much time it took to prepare such a note and what would happen if the tax collector did not come, the bemused citizens could only offer a harassed look. It was unbelievable that for something as fundamental as paying taxes there was such an intimidating arrangement. Something had to be done to change all that.

Another worrying scenario was that of many people visiting the commissioner daily for the delivery of basic services like drinking water, street lighting or sanitation and endlessly waiting for the authorities to meet their demands. The system had to be comprehensively reformed and Information and Communications Technology offered the easiest and the most cost-effective solution. It was then that the idea of such a project which could help meet the basic needs of citizens took shape. This was followed by brainstorming sessions with all the stakeholders to get to the root of the problem. A core team was put into place for data computerisation and software and hardware support. The search for private entrepreneurs ready to invest as stakeholders in the project was driven by the paucity of funds. This became a catalyst for the early completion of the project.

The name Saukaryam was chosen as it meant 'facility' in the local language. The name was considered apt for the project as it was supposed to provide wide ranging facilities to the citizens. Naming the project in the people's language would also bring it closer to their hearts. Work on the project began in right earnest and a deadline of two months was given to all the partners. Development of the website was the most critical aspect and it had to be done by making the office team sit for long sessions with the developer. The website had to be refined from the users point of view and given a new and un-government like feature. The networking also took time as it had to be done across the length and breadth of the city. Testing and data encryption proceeded simultaneously. Everything finally came about together on the day when the project was formally inaugurated by the chief minister of the state. In the following months many changes took place in the project. Not only were new services added but the number of service centres also multiplied gradually. The response citizens have never felt better about their lives than they are doing now. However, the project still has a long way to go.

CONCLUSION

Effective government-citizen interaction holds the key to good governance. Information Technology can play a crucial role in improving this interaction. This has been successfully tried in project Saukaryam, which has brought in transparency, accountability and speedy delivery of civic services in Vishakhapatnam. The project's website and the City Service Centre have streamlined filing and settlement of complaints and grievances, tracking of building plans, registration of births and deaths, monitoring of garbage lifting and other infrastructure works. Now at the click of the mouse, the citizens can see the progress of all infrastructure works being enacted in the city.

E-governance by Information Technology: Initiatives of a Metropolitan City

— **Vijay Rattan**

INTRODUCTION

The concept of e-governance is of recent origin in Information Technology (IT). This emerging concept has brought about a paradigm shift in IT usage and applications for good governance. It attempts to take public services and the government, literally to the doorstep of the citizens through IT. E-governance facilitates the delivery of government services to the masses through procedural simplicity, speed and convenience.

E-governance is also seen as a multi-dimensional concept, an IT driven methodology that improves efficiency in administration, brings about transparency and leads to the reduction of costs in running the government. There are three main domains of e-governance: improving governmental processes (e-administration); connecting citizens (e-citizens and e-services); and building external interactions (e-society).

Richard Heeks points out that governance is both, the present and the future of developing countries like India, which still have a long way to go. Currently, more than half of India's villages lack telephone connectivity, let alone Internet access. The 26 million phone lines (mostly business-owned) and 2 million Internet subscribers that do exist nationwide are concentrated in urban areas, while rural areas are left out of the loop.

E-GOVERNANCE

E-governance has emerged because of the increasing interest of governments and citizens around the world to experiment with and learn to exploit new media and the latest technologies. It involves new styles of leadership, new ways of debating and deciding policy and investment, accessing education, listening to citizens and organising and delivering information and services.

E-governance and e-government initiatives now enable citizens to access government documents, order publications, file taxes, order vital records, and renew licences and permits from any location with an Internet connection. In addition, there are already signs that e-government is transforming organisations by breaking down organisational boundaries and providing greater access to information, enhancing communication and facilitating democratic processes.

Another term used for e-governance is *digital governance*. Digital governance is a way to ensure that common citizens have equal right to be a part of decision-making processes, which affect them directly or indirectly, and influence them in a manner which best improves their conditions and the quality of their lives. The new form of governance will ensure that citizens are no longer passive consumers of services offered to them, and would transform them to play a decisive role in deciding the kind of services they want and the structures that could best provide the same.

Governments in developing countries have been using IT for more than 40 years, so what's new about e-governance? Richard Heeks answers this question by saying that we are moving on from IT to Information and Communication Technology (ICT) and from IT to Information Society (IS). The old model was of IT, providing automation to the internal workings of government by data processing, whereas the shift is to a new model of Information and Communication Technologies (ICT) that support and transform the external workings of governance by processing and communicating data. From a focus on processing applications (i.e. computers, the I in ICT), to a focus on communications (i.e. networks, the C in ICT), the focus has now shifted to both processing and communications. As the power and reach of ICT grow, so does the power and reach of change in governments. A final trend is the move of ICT from within to outside of governments.

Further, e-governance should be seen to encompass all ICT, but the key innovation is computer networks. These include creating a wealth of new digital connections in terms of connections within the government to permit 'joined-up thinking', connections between government and NGOs/ citizens to strengthen accountability, connections between government and business/citizens to transform service delivery, connections within and between NGOs to support learning and concerted action, and connections within and between communities for socio-economic development. As a result, the focus grows from just e-administration to include e-citizens, e-services and e-society. Overall, then, e-governance is the ICT enabled route to achieving good governance.

E-governance enables good governance by way of:

Automation. Involving replacement of current manual processes, which involve collecting, storing, processing, and transmitting information by automation.

Information. Supporting current processes of decision-making, communication and implementation of decisions.

Transformation. Creating new methods of public service delivery.

These bring the following gains to governance strategies:

Efficiency Gains

- Governance that is cheaper and produces the same output at lower total cost.
- Governance that does more, i.e. produces more output at the same total cost.
- Governance that is quicker, producing the same output, at the same total costs, in less time.

Effectiveness Gains

- Governance that works better, producing the same output at the same total cost, in the same time, but of a higher quality.
- Governance that is innovative, producing new output.

These gains lead to better staff morale, effective political control and improved public image for the government.

E-GOVERNANCE IN CHANDIGARH

Chandigarh, with a population of over 9 lakh, is considered to be India's best planned city. A comprehensive IT policy for the city, which has one of the highest literacy rates in the country, was released on April 29, 2000. The Action Plan for the policy is given in Annexure I. The policy was formulated to tap the growing potential of IT for development. It envisions technological benefits to be made available to every person in Chandigarh, in the next five years. A proposal to make Chandigarh an e-governed city is under way with three projects, viz. Employee Information System, Hospital Management, and Engineering Works Monitoring, which has been sent to C-DAC initially.

The IT policy aims to provide public services, promote industry and business, reduce unemployment, increase software exports and, above all, improve the quality of life of the people by the use of Information and Communication Technology. It also focuses on human resource development, creation of IT infrastructure and development of IT industry in Chandigarh. Significantly, the mission is to strive to make Chandigarh an ideal IT destination by providing public service for the residents through efficient, speedy and cost-effective e-governance.

An Advisory Committee on IT Applications has been set up (the composition of the advisory committee is given in Annexure II) the purpose of which is to provide a vision and direction to the IT Implementation Committee so as to achieve the aims and objectives of the IT policy.

Steps have been initiated to develop Chandigarh as a 'wired city', by setting up software development units, use of intelligent network service, information centres/kiosks, Internet service providers (ISPs)/gateway with provision of real time connectivity to international gateways and Internet access through cable TV network. Departments of Health and Agriculture are enlightening the people in rural areas about the utility of IT services.

To facilitate easy access to government offices, a Committee for Implementation has been set up. The composition of this committee is given in Annexure III. A task force has also been set up in each department to oversee the implementation of the policy. The composition of the task force is given in Annexure IV.

E-GOVERNANCE MEASURES FOR IMPROVING INTERNAL ADMINISTRATION

The following measures have been taken for the application of e-governance:

Budget

The budgetary provision for IT has been increased to 30% from 1%. This includes investment in IT hardware, software, services and training.

LAN/WAN

To increase efficiency under the IT policy, it is aimed to establish local area network and wide area network to intra-connect and inter-connect the Secretariat with all other government offices. Personal computers, e-mail and fax facilities are being provided to senior government officers. A local area network, (LAN) has been set up in the Secretariat and video conferencing on web cams has been started. Wide area network (WAN) is being set up. The Chandigarh secretariat, secretariats of Punjab and Haryana, Estate Office, and the Punjab and Haryana High Court have also been linked.

The administration has signed an agreement with all the cable laying companies for providing free bandwidth. An IT park, spread over 104 acres is being set up with private collaboration.

File Management

At various levels of each department and public service undertaking, an automated and transparent file movement system has been introduced.

Training of Personnel

Senior officers are trained by the Society for Promotion of IT in Chandigarh (SPIC) at the Microsoft Centre of Excellence, set up at the local Punjab Engineering College.

Awards

As an incentive to encourage IT usage, the IT policy provides for awards to be given to those departments/public sector undertakings (PSUs), which show outstanding performance in IT. Committees have been set up for the selection of awardees in the field of software exports and e-governance.

E-GOVERNANCE MEASURES TO IMPROVE THE CITIZEN-ADMINISTRATION INTERFACE

The following measures have been taken by different departments/agencies:

Information Facilitation Centres

An information facilitation centre with touch screen input facility is functional in the secretariat and one more is coming up in the Central State Library. Such centres and information kiosks are to be set up throughout the city.

Excise and Taxation Department

Modifications and improvements are being brought about in the implementation of the system of taxation prevailing in the union territory. Online submission of forms has started in the excise department. Online connectivity enables simplified procedures for levying of commercial taxes, thus eliminating delays and bottlenecks in the taxation procedures. A database of registered dealers is being maintained. Steps are on for computerising the issuance of licences and automatic updating of STV registers. This would also enable automatic generation of notices, defaulters and pending payments.

Education Department

All colleges and schools are to be fully computerised and all students encouraged to be IT literate. All educational institutions including medical and engineering colleges are to be connected online with the education department.

Municipal Corporation

All services provided by the municipal corporation are being computerised. Citizens will be able to access various departments of the corporation online from kiosks to be set up throughout the city. Public grievances are to be given priority and resolved speedily by the use of computers and inter-connectivity. In this regard, work is in progress on a public management information system complaint website.

Estate Office

The Estate Office is to provide information to all residents through terminals to be set up throughout the city. Procedures are being simplified through the use of computers and inter-connectivity. Forms and instructions are already available online to the general public through the citys website. Except certain documents which have to remain confidential, all files of the Estate Office are to be computerised.

Driving Licences and Registration

Issuance of driving licences and registration certificates has been computerised and the procedures for renewal have also been made convenient through online connectivity. A scheme for introducing smart cards for registration certificates and driving licences is already under way.

Treasury

The government treasury is being computerised and connected online with the secretariat and other important offices. Manual processes are being minimised and all bills and other documents are being computerised.

Police

Chandigarh police personnel are being made computer literate. For ensuring greater efficiency, the secretariat and the police headquarters are also being connected online for speedy communication and exchange of information. The police headquarters are to be connected with the police stations and also to the office of the District Magistrate and the Subdivisional Magistrate.

Website

A website, *http://www:chandigarh.nic.in* has been launched to provide detailed sector-wise maps of the city for the convenience of the public. Besides, there are separate websites of the Chandigarh Police, Department of IT, and the Government Medical College and Hospital.

CONCLUSION

E-governance is an emerging mode of administration and delivering services to people by the utilisation of Information and Communication Technologies. Besides, dealing with the role and importance of e-governance, an attempt is made to highlight IT innovations in the city of Chandigarh. The IT policy, which came into being in April 2000, envisages the setting up of an IT infrastructure, development of human resources, besides making e-governance possible. Connectivity among the departments has been established through the local area network and wide area network. Likewise, facilitation counters at various offices and computerisation of various services like registration of vehicles and the availability of application forms has facilitated the delivery of services to the citizens.

REFERENCES

1. Bong, Mark, *The IT Global Revolution*, 2000.
2. Chandigarh Administration, *Smartcity-Chandigarh*, March–April 2001.
3. Department of Information Technology (UT), Chandigarh Administration, *IT Policy of Union Territory of Chandigarh*, April 2000.
4. Heeks, Richard, 'Understanding e-governance for development, government working paper', *Series Working Paper No. 11*, Institute for Development Policy and Management, 2001, University of Manchester.
5. Nath, Vikas, *Networks for Empowerment and Governance*, 2000.
6. Prabhu, C.S.R., *Collectorate*, Government of India, Ministry of Information Technology, NIC, Hyderabad, 2000.
7. Madan Mohan, Rao, *E-governance Services to Unleash Billion Dollar Market in India*, 2001.

Annexure I

IMPLEMENTATION OF INFORMATION TECHNOLOGY AND E-GOVERNANCE IN UNION TERRITORY, CHANDIGARH

Action Plan

Analysis

1. Identify the departments which have public interaction.
2. Identify the existing functional modes in each department.
3. Identify the department's level of interface with the public and with other departments.
4. Identify the existing manpower with respect to IT skills.
5. Identify the required skill levels for proper public interface.

6. Identify the training models required for smooth interface and gradual changeover to e-governance.
7. Identify the training schedules/schemes.

Design

1. Design basic network services to be provided in the city.
2. Design the departmental infrastructure.
3. Design the public interfaces.
4. Identify organisations for setting up such facilities.

Implementation

1. Select priority services to be made functional through e-governance.
2. Select priority areas to be networked.
3. Select priority departments.
4. Implement the plan.
5. Monitoring.
6. Review.
7. Make an efficient and functional e-governance model.
8. Implement the model throughout the union territory.

Annexure II

ADVISORY COMMITTEE FOR IT APPLICATION

The Committee meets once in a quarter. It consists of:

1. Advisor to Administrator, Chairperson.
2. Finance Secretary and Secretary IT, Vice-Chairperson.
3. Home Secretary, Member.
4. Commissioner Chandigarh Municipal Corporation, Member.
5. Deputy Commissioner, Member.
6. Joint Secretary Finance, Director Public Instruction ©, Member.
7. Managing Director, CITCO, Member.
8. Inspector General of Police, Member.
9. Chief Engineer, UT, Member.
10. Principal General Manager Telecom, Member.
11. Director Regional Computer Centre, Member.
12. Additional Director STPI, Member.
13. Director IT, Member.
14. Director Health, Member.
15. Director Technical Education, Member.
16. State Informatics Officer, National Informatics Centre, Member.
17. Additional Director IT, Member, Convenor.

Annexure III

IT IMPLEMENTATION COMMITTEE

The IT Implementation Committee monitors the progress of the Departmental Task Forces to implement the decisions/guidelines of the Advisory Committee. The purpose of this committee is to carry forward the vision and direction of the Advisory Committee and get it implemented through the task forces. It also coordinates the working of the task forces.

The Committee meets once in every two months. It consists of the following members:

1. Finance Secretary and Secretary IT, Chairman.
2. Commissioner Chandigarh Municipal Corporation, Vice-Chairman.
3. Deputy Commissioner, Member.
4. Senior Superintendent of Police, Member.
5. Chief Engineer, Member.
6. Sub-Divisional Magistrate (South), Member.
7. Director Public Instruction (Schools), Member
8. Assistant Estate Officer, Member.
9. Director IT, Member.
10. State Informatics Officer, National Informatics Centre, Member.
11. Under Secretary IT, Member.
12. Deputy Excise and Taxation Commissioner, Member.
13. Additional Director IT, Member, Convenor.

Annexure IV

IT TASK FORCE

Task forces have been set up in various departments, for the implementation of the IT policy in that department. The task force meets at least once a month to monitor the progress of the department's IT plan. Each task force submits periodic reports to the IT Implementation Committee.

The task force consists of the following:

1. Head of the Department (HOD), Chairman.
2. Nodal Officer.
3. Representative of NIC.
4. Representative of IT Department.

Issues and Strategies in Good Governance with Special Reference to Karnataka

— Vivek Kulkarni

INTRODUCTION

India has emerged as an IT superpower in the last ten years. The 1991 World Bank Survey gave India 26 points and Ireland 27 points for IT capability. After 10 years, another study by NASSCOM-McKinsey placed India far ahead of Ireland in terms of vendor and people satisfaction.

The Software Engineering Institute (SEI), at the Carnegie Mellon University, rates software companies using its Capability Maturity Model (CMM) and assigns ratings from Level 1 to Level 5. This model was developed by SEI for Pentagon, the US Department of Defense. This standard-setting institute gives Level 5 to extremely productive companies that write error free software, have excellent human resources and follow rigorous quality control processes. The world over, there are only 40 companies that have been awarded CMM Level 5. Of those, 29 are located in India. Thus, almost 75 per cent of the world's best IT companies are located in India.

Even though India is an IT superpower, good governance is a must for achieving the development objectives. Good governance has to be provided by both the central and state governments. The country must, however, quickly liberalise its infrastructure areas, particularly telecommunication, and supply of manpower. This chapter discusses all the issues and strategies in governance, especially in the perspective of IT.

ISSUES IN GOVERNANCE

There are a number of issues that need to be resolved quickly. A few critical ones are discussed here.

Delay

Age old procedures, a legacy left by the British, are the primary reason for delayed government decisions. Though the British have changed these procedures and brought about important and modern civil services reforms in their country, it is somewhat annoying that we continue to follow the old procedures with no change whatsoever.

For instance, consider how files are handled in the secretariat. Many files begin with the junior assistant and travel all the way up to the cabinet ministers. There are several layers in between—assistant, senior assistant, section officer, under secretary, deputy secretary, joint secretary, additional secretary, secretary, principal secretary, minister of state and the cabinet minister. Thus, the file has to pass through 9 to 12 layers. Assume that each layer takes exactly two working days to clear the file. This reasonable assumption often turns out wrong much to the chagrin of citizens. By the time the file goes up and then returns to the assistant's level, it can take about 36 working days or two months. However, if queries are raised at any level, the file goes down and is put up again, even though the relevant information may be in the file. This implies double layers and a delay of four months. In case, someone decides that the finance department's opinion has to be sought, the file has to travel yet another set of nine layers. That means, six months for a routine decision. A common joke (which can be a bitter reality for some) in the secretariat is 'lose the file to the law department if you don't want to take any decision.' Information Technology can considerably reduce these delays.

Comprehensiveness

Quite often, government work expands according to the number of employees. For instance, compare security checking in any Indian airport with that of an airport in a foreign country. In most foreign airports, passengers as well as visitors can go up to the boarding gate. All visitors are checked once by the security and asked to put down all their cell phones, keys, coins, etc., in a small tray and made to walk through the metal detector. If the metal detector does not beep, they can just cross the gates. At Indian airports, whenever there is a security alert, visitors are not allowed. This can be very worrying if, for instance, the visitor has to see off an aged family member. For passengers too, the security check means a number of security personnel touching them even after passing through the metal detector. In addition, the x-rayed baggage is opened and repeatedly checked. This is because there are so many security personnel and everyone needs to be given a task. That is how the government works, according to and in proportion to the number of employees who already exist.

Complexity

Government departments are compartmentalised and do not want to be connected and work together. Several instances have been reported where the police could have caught the criminals had they acted on the complaints of citizens. Police stations have refused to register serious complaints saying they do not come under their jurisdiction. The police do not act and also do not inform the concerned police station themselves. They want the citizen to call the station. However, the geographical distribution is very confusing in cities and people may not know which police station handles which area.

Another example is that of the customs department. If you import a computer from a foreign country and try to get clearance from the said department, you will never know whom to approach first and no one will demystify the procedures for you. The department makes you visit each and every clerk. There could have been just one person to take the papers and finally deliver the product but that never happens. This inefficiency compels people to use the services of agents.

The government usually buys low quality goods at very high cost. The primary reason for this is the complexity of the tendering process. Most often, the lowest price bid is accepted. The quality is usually not properly defined. Reputed companies prefer to avoid participating in government tenders. They would rather deal with big private sector companies, where they can negotiate, compete and get quick payments. Even when they participate in government tenders, they build in a premium for delays and uncertainties. Says Steve Dempsey, the e-government specialist of Anderson Consulting:

> ... The government tenders often run to 1000 pages, and picking the winner can take 18 months. Then the contract can become a battleground as both sides take out frustrations on each other. Often the government department deserves blame for poor management, but vendors too must take their share for over promising and under bidding. They, in turn, would argue that this happens because public servants tend to award tenders on the basis of price rather than value, quality or past performance.

STRATEGIES IN GOVERNANCE

Even though the scenario looks grim, it is possible to make the government work effectively. The strategies should focus on four areas. First, the government should go for structural changes and decentralise power in a big way. Economic growth is the second requirement. Third, public-private partnership must be encouraged. Finally, Information Technology should be used to usher effective e-governance.

Decentralise Power

Even though we have been talking of decentralisation for the last 50 years, actually a lot of centralisation has happened. Consider our municipal corporations today. They offer poor water supply and hospitals, and do not maintain roads. The rich and the middle class shun municipal schools. A few decades ago municipal schools were run quite well and municipal corporations maintained electric utilities. In China, an official of the rank of mayor can give you clearances on the spot. In sharp contrast to this, mayors of our cities have limited authority and need to go to the chief minister and present a memorandum for more funds. Our municipal and other local bodies should be strengthened and the Centre should let power flow to cities and districts. The same applies to the states too.

The government should gradually start simplifying its rules and outsource its activities wherever possible. The government could keep for itself core activities like currency, defence, external affairs, law and order, and social services for the socially backward. But there are many other roles, such as the financing and laying of roads, financing and privatising the power projects, etc. which the government can easily outsource to the private sector. This can save a lot of government funds. The government can then concentrate on the core activities.

Economic Growth

India is well placed to take advantage of knowledge-based sectors. We must liberalise all sectors immediately if we are to make a difference. Even though the telecom sector has been liberalised, much needs to be done. China for instance, has been adding 2.5 million telephone connections every year, which is equivalent to India's cumulative total. In other words, in a year China adds a little India to itself in terms of Internet connectivity.

The second problem is the monopolistic condition. For instance, the VSNL prices an T_1 line for about Rs. 40 lakh in Mumbai, and Rs. 75 lakh in cities like Bangalore and Hyderabad. It is important that rates are brought down considerably. Calculations on the basis of data from the IT Task Force in Bangalore show that it is possible to offer an T_1 line for as low as Rs. 1.8 lakh in Bangalore. If this is done, everyone will go for broadband connections. Knowledge-based sectors will leapfrog and put the country in the top ranks.

Public-private Partnership

An excellent experiment in this direction is taking place in Karnataka. The government has involved several private sector professionals and academicians in task forces, who not only advise it on policy matters but also help in implementation. The Chief Minister's IT Task Force includes experts from private IT firms like Infosys, Vision Group, etc. Such collaborative efforts enrich government policies.

E-governance

Information Technology is advancing beyond our expectations. Hardware power doubles every 18 months thereby confirming Moore's law. The cost of 1 Mhz processing power was $7600 in 1970. Today, it has come down to 17 cents. In 1860s, a 20-word telegram cost Rs. 64,600. Today a 20-page document can be e-mailed for less than 50 paise. Many old and new economy firms are taking advantage of IT to improve their productivity. For instance, Dell reduced its inventory from 150 days to only 15 days using IT. Even governments can take advantage of this technology. The procedures and rules can be notified on the web. In addition, every department must be encouraged to give out as much information as possible on regularly updated web site.

E-governance should first operate in departments that matter to citizens. There are several successful examples of such initiatives. For instance, computer assisted registration (CARDS) has made buying stamps and registering property sale documents easier in Andhra Pradesh. Then, networking and connectivity projects in Dhar, Warana Nagar and Himachal Pradesh have introduced simple digital economics in the villages. E-governance projects must be taken up for maintaining land records of farmers, registration of personal properties, payment of electricity bills etc. In fact, e-governance projects need to be taken up in utility payment areas.

IT INITIATIVES IN KARNATAKA

IT initiatives in Karnataka aim to provide direct citizen interface, improve human resources and connectivity, and improve the efficiency of government officials. IT has been applied in the following areas.

Common Entrance Test

Karnataka has numerous institutions of higher education and attracts students from other Indian states and countries. Every year the state conducts the common entrance test. Over 150,000 students take the exams and around 50 per cent are from outside the state. The entire admission process is absolutely transparent. The fact that students from outside the state participate in large numbers shows their confidence in the local administration. Before computerisation, the process attracted many questions from elected representatives and a lot of litigation. Now the system is so transparent that it has rid itself of both.

Education Department

The 240,000 government teachers receive their salary via computerised pay bills and bank accounts. Even the recruitment of teachers has now been computerised. The state has appointed over 80,000 teachers through computerised recruitment. Even the transfers of teachers are done through a computerised counselling process. 1000 schools all over the state have full fledged computer laboratories with the most modern computers, Internet and faculty from prominent training firms like Aptech, NIIT etc.

Mukhya Vahini

This is the chief minister's decision support system. Presently, it tracks the CM's instructions, the projects sanctioned under the Global Investor Meet, the constituency management system, summarised data on major projects in health, housing and other social sector schemes. Many modules are already in use.

Bhoomi and Nondani

Bhoomi is the state's computerised land records project. It aims to cover 60 lakh farmers in 175 *taluks*. Presently it is operational in 48 *taluks*. *Nondani* is computerised registration, operational in 12 sub-registration offices in Bangalore. It accounts for about 40 per cent of the total revenue.

Secretariat Local Area Network (LAN)

This envisages computerisation of all secretariat departments. It enables citizens to know the status of their files and the number of days they took to be cleared at various stages.

Khajane

This Rs. 45 crores project is in an advanced stage of implementation. The system keeps accounts for all payments of the state, which totals to approximately Rs. 24,000 crores a year. Besides government payments, the system makes payments to 6 lakh employees, 3 lakh pensioners, 13 lakh aged, widowed and handicapped pensioners. The accounts, available real time, are stored in data centres in Bangalore and a disaster centre in Dharwad. The STPI is the network partner. The major benefit of the project is the instantaneous reconciliation of government accounts. In addition, the system displays the money spent on all government schemes in every village. This enhances transparency and improves quality.

E-lottery

The government has floated a tender to set up 10,000 terminals all over the state. Apart from running the electronic lottery, the kiosks could be used to disseminate other public information.

Yuva.com

This programme envisages 225 training centres all over the state run by prestigious firms like Aptech, NIIT, SSI, etc. The fees in the centre are already reduced. The government gives subsidy of Rs. 1500 for a three-month course. A maximum subsidy of Rs. 4500 is offered for a six-month course. The programme aims to train over 100,000 rural youths in a year. Over 100 centres are operational at present.

Other Initiatives

The Commercial Tax Department tracks goods using check-post entries. Information about movement of goods is automatically put in the dealers' assessment file. In terms of tax collection per GDP, the state is one of the best in India. The Insurance Department uses computers to track all the government vehicle insurance details. Police salary bills are computerised. The Irrigation Department has a major project on e-tendering and e-procurement. Silk trading exchange in Karnataka has been computerised since 1985.

CONCLUSION

Presently India, is an IT superpower and can play a vital role in the knowledge based global economy. Almost 75 per cent of the world's best IT companies are in India. The growth can produce millions of jobs not only in the IT sector but also in several supporting service sectors. This can transform an agricultural economy into a vibrant, service based one. However, laxity in decision-making, compartmentalisation of government departments, complexities of tenders and misuse of funds in procuring hardware are the main obstacles which have to be overcome.

This chapter identifies strategies in four key areas, which can help India achieve its goal. Firstly, decentralisation of power would reduce delays in decision making and make every agency/department more accountable. Secondly, economic growth would automatically introduce newer and better services for the citizen. Thirdly, public-private partnership would help make the government more efficient. Lastly, e-governance initiatives would help make governance more easy and citizen-friendly.

FRIENDS: An E-governance Project of Kerala

— **Aruna Sunderarajan**

INTRODUCTION

As good governance today often connotes effective e-governance, every type of novel e-governance venture must be able to address certain basic queries. How can the benefits of e-governance immediately be made available to citizens in developing countries when the comprehensive induction of Information Technology (IT) in government is complex, time consuming and expensive? Is it desirable to set up computerised, front-end interface for the common person to access public services, without waiting for back-end computerisation? How critical are the attitudes and the motivation levels of the project staff for the success of an e-governance project?

These issues were addressed in an extraordinarily successful project in Kerala where an IT enabled, single-window, front-end interface called FRIENDS (Fast, Reliable, Instant, Efficient, Network for Disbursement of Services) was set up for availing a range of popular public services like payment of taxes and utility charges, and renewal of licences without waiting for back-end computerisation or systems integration in the government. In the span of one year, this project has expanded to serve 13 million people in 12 of the 14 districts in Kerala.

APPLICATION OF THE PROJECT

Each FRIENDS centre receives almost 1000 visitors everyday and users are delighted with the service levels. The average waiting time is ten minutes and transactions are completed in three to five minutes. Unlike most government offices, the ambience here is pleasant, and the service is courteous and corruption-free. The citizen is made to feel wanted. The project, likely to receive ISO certification soon, has been a success largely because of its focus on training and motivating the employees manning these centres. It also features an innovative public-private partnership with the involvement of poor women's groups, which undertake supplemental services.

Usually, a citizen in Kerala has to interact with at least eight to ten government departments/agencies for accessing routine services. Traditional payment systems necessitate visiting each of these government offices and waiting in tedious queues. Some transactions take as long as a day to be completed. Often staff are rude and sometimes bribes are demanded through touts and intermediaries. The poor public perception of the government arises from these unpleasant experiences.

In 1999, the state government set up an Information Technology Mission Group to selectively induct IT in areas and departments where it could provide immediate and tangible benefits to citizens. This was envisaged as a necessary prelude to the comprehensive induction of IT across the government. It was anticipated that IT-enabled services would find widespread acceptance, given the near 100 per cent literacy levels, and the vibrancy of social and community life in Kerala. The state has recently undertaken a major structural reform programme of devolution of power to local governments. The e-governance initiative has been envisaged as a major component of this decentralisation process.

A New Approach

The philosophy of FRIENDS is to treat the citizen, who is paying for the services, as a valued customer, who must be given the respect that he or she deserves. The underlying concept is simple—to provide an integrated electronic interface whereby citizens can remit taxes, pay bills, access commonly required government services and obtain the latest information on government programmes. It was decided to focus on front-end computerisation, rather than await the completion of back-end computerisation of these departments, to make these services immediately available. The pilot project was launched in Thiruvananthapuram in June 2000. On the basis of its success, the project was extended to other districts.

At FRIENDS, 20 computerised counters work from 9 A.M. to 7 P.M. on all days of the week, in an 'any service-any counter' mode. A computerised queue management system eliminates queues, and customers receive a token and await their turn in a pleasant setting. The services offered are free. Payments can be made in cash or by demand draft. A help desk is on hand for any required assistance. The centre works on the principle of 'collect and remit' and 'receive and forward', by interacting with the concerned departments/agencies. Eventually, the computers at the centre will be linked with the servers of the departments on a 'real time' basis, once the back-end computerisation is completed.

FRIENDS counters are equipped to handle more than 1000 kinds of bills or documents. The software is robust enough to handle these requirements and new modules can be incorporated when new departments/ services are added. The indicative list of the services offered by the FRIENDS counters are: water and power utility payments, bill payments, property tax, professional tax, traders licence fee, building tax, land tax, revenue recovery, fee for new ration card, one time vehicle tax, motor vehicle tax, etc.

A customised software package has been developed for FRIENDS with a robust and effective database at the back-end and a user-friendly front-end. The software has been developed with ASP, Windows 2000 and SQL RDBMS. Transactions are secured by firewalls, and reports can be generated in line with the MIS requirements of the participating departments. The services provided by FRIENDS are proposed to be web-enabled in the next phase and discussions are under way for creating payment gateways for this purpose.

A notable feature of the project is that its personnel have been drawn from the participating departments, and no new jobs have been created. There are 50 staff members in each centre, and 500 people have thus been inducted. An innovative feature of the project is the employment opportunity it provides to poor women from self-help groups, who manage the helpdesks and provide supplementary services.

IMPLEMENTATION CHALLENGES

Breaking Down Departmental Barriers

Ensuring the active participation of various departments has been one of the most difficult challenges in this project. Initially, most departments viewed the project as an initiative of the IT department and were unwilling to delegate their functions to the centre. Moreover, many of these functions were sources of irregular lucrative earnings for the departmental staff, hence, they were reluctant to forego them. Periodic interactions were held with the departments and nodal officers, and efforts were made to address the concerns of departments. Traditionally, departments were extremely wary of collaborating with other departments but the pilot project at Thiruvananthapuram managed to break through these barriers. When the project was expanded to other districts, the departments showed a far greater degree of enthusiasm for participation and came up with creative suggestions for improvement.

Computerising the Front-end without Back-end Computerisation

While the government had embarked on a comprehensive programme of computerising all major departments, it was realised that this would be complex and time consuming, requiring a complete overhaul of existing systems. After considerable debate, it was decided to start with front-end computerisation, rather than wait for full-fledged automation, and to begin with the minimal required procedural changes, which were a prerequisite for the project. Since complete online data transfer is a critical component of the FRIENDS project, departmental computerisation plans were also revised to accord priority to this.

BENEFITS AND COSTS

The most dramatic impact of FRIENDS project has been the change in citizens' perception about the government. Moreover, visitors have been impressed by the courteous and corruption-free atmosphere. FRIENDS has also demonstrated that ordinary government functionaries and poor women can deliver high-quality services in an atmosphere of excellence. The demonstration value of this project is inestimable. An unforeseen, but key outcome is that FRIENDS has succeeded in providing positive feedback on the benefits of inducting IT in all the participating departments.

The capital cost of each FRIENDS centre is Rs. 2 million and the annual recurring expenditure is around Rs. 0.7 million. FRIENDS does not levy service charges, and costs are presently shared by participating departments. However, it is proposed to make these centres self-sustaining by levying nominal service charges, and by providing other chargeable business and commercial services.

Recently, the FRIENDS centres have tied up with Bharat Sanchar Nigam Ltd (BSNL) to accept telecom payments. The BSNL shall pay a nominal sum calculated on the basis of the number of transactions effected as service charge to the FRIENDS centres. This facility is expected to benefit 22 lakh consumers in the state. Payment of insurance premium has also been introduced in the centres. It is expected that the revenues generated by this arrangement will be sufficient to cover the recurring expenditure of the centres.

KEY LESSONS

The Quality of Service Matters, Not the Level of Technology

While making technology choices the government has a tendency to opt for complex, state-of-the-art systems, with the result that IT induction is often perceived as expensive and complicated. In Kerala, a number of such projects have been underway for years, without significant results. FRIENDS is not a complex or high-technology project, but it proves that simple technologies, if creatively used, can dramatically improve the delivery of services.

For Optimal Results, Start from the Front-end

When this project was being considered questions were raised about the basic wisdom of embarking on IT induction at the front-end without comprehensive back-end computerisation. However, complete back-end computerisation is a long drawn process. The project has shown that while inducting IT into the government, it may be useful, to start from the front-end, because partial solutions like this can yield significant efficiency gains with modest levels of investment.

The Key Factor is Motivated Manpower

In the absence of horizontal mobility, departmental compartmentalisation is very high. It is also generally felt that staff at the lower levels of administration are unresponsive and even shirk work. Moreover, IT has always been viewed with suspicion and distrust. In the 80s, government employees had launched agitations against computerisation. The challenge was to run the project with this kind of staff. Moreover, most of the staff had very little computer knowledge. The strategy was to impart the feeling that the individuals selected for FRIENDS had a very special responsibility and this was the focus of the training programme. Besides, special care was taken to ensure that the ambience provided was superior to the normal working environs and the point was driven home that this ambience had been created not just to impress the customers but also because the staff were very special.

The result was that the staff felt that if they behaved pleasantly, the customers would be happy. Their self-esteem went up substantially as they perceived themselves as computer professionals working in a superior environment and trying to satisfy the customers. Almost all the staff members brought their families and showed them how they were working in a modern work environment. Today, the biggest asset of FRIENDS is its dedicated manpower that has transcended departmental barriers. The additional training offered has convinced them that they are indeed being looked upon as resource persons and many have started learning computer skills on their own. They are also acting as champions for IT in their own parent departments.

The Virtues of Starting Small

Since IT was viewed with distrust by a majority of the government staff, it was imperative to undertake a small pilot project in an area where the benefits to all the stakeholders would be immediately visible. The success of FRIENDS has enhanced the demand from the public for IT-enabled services, and has also eased the way for the introduction of other IT projects in the government.

Public-private Partnerships in IT

One of the most interesting aspects of the project has been the involvement of self-help women's groups from families below the poverty line. They were brought in to render support services in the FRIENDS centres. These groups offer services such as fax and call centres; run refreshment centres and man the help desks, particularly for poor and semi-literate clients. The government staff and these women have bonded as a team. This is the first project in Kerala, where such an unconventional partnership has succeeded in providing high-quality services. After obtaining specialised training and experience, these women are now ready to take on a larger role in the running of the centres. A proposal to franchise similar centres to these groups is under consideration.

CONCLUSION

Information Technology can simplify administrative procedures and bring in umpteen benefits. A front-end interface for the common man to access public services without full-fledged back-end computerisation has been successfully brought about by the innovative FRIENDS project. The project has provided a network for disbursement of services. FRIENDS centres have been planned to become self-sustaining, full-fledged, public-private partnerships, eventually delivering a multiple range of online services. These will become widely dispersed public access points for IT enabled services which are subject to independent quality monitoring and audit.

Governance for Development: New Initiative Gramsat Pilot Project, Orissa

— S.P. Nanda

INTRODUCTION

The concept of development for people's welfare, which is aimed at improving their quality of life, has gone through several changes in the last few decades. As a parameter of development, the equitable distribution of wealth among various sections of society has taken precedence over Gross Domestic Product (GDP). In due course of time, emphasis has been laid on total literacy, health for all, a crime and stress free life. In recent times, religious and communal intolerance has become a serious threat. Therefore, secular and harmonious living is gaining importance in the development agenda of governance. Human rights and freedom are now regarded as important aspects of development. Governance is the process by which a state implements policies, which affect the public. In the context of development, good governance is necessary to ensure that various development programmes are carried out successfully.

This chapter deals with development issues and the strategies adopted to benefit society, economy and all regions of the state. One important initiative taken by the Government of Orissa under the Gramsat pilot project has also been discussed.

DEVELOPMENT ISSUES

In discharging its role of governance for development, the state is faced with the issues of directing the benefits of development to all sections of the society, to all sectors of the economy and to all regions of the state. In order to achieve these goals, development schemes are conceived keeping in mind various target groups of the society and different sectors of the economy. Development programmes such as the crop insurance and financing for irrigation wells (bore-wells/dug-wells) under the Million Well Scheme are examples of schemes directed towards benefitting the farming community. Providing improved seeds, making available fertilisers and pesticides at the appropriate time during the crop-growing season and also ensuring minimum support price for agricultural produce are some of the efforts made by the government towards improving the economic standards of farmers. Similarly, there are schemes for landless labourers. Normally, such labourers are engaged in agricultural and other activities available in their locality. When drought or flood affects an area, the government introduces schemes under the Food for Work Programme—creating infrastructure and community assets such as roads, ponds, tanks, plantations, etc.—which create local employment opportunities. There are also special provisions and programmes for village artisans like weavers, carpenters, rope makers and the manufacturers of household articles. In order to improve the educational level of the population, a basic indicator of quality of life, the government has started the Literacy Mission.

There are special schemes of preventive medical care to address certain endemic diseases and mass immunisation programmes for the elimination of certain diseases. There are special schemes for women and children. Backward communities like scheduled castes and scheduled tribes are covered under special schemes. Physically disabled and old people are given special allowances and special consideration for employment on humanitarian grounds. Since poverty is a self-perpetuating phenomenon, there are special schemes for people below the poverty line. These include providing houses and special financial assistance to develop some means of sustainable livelihood so as to make the poor self-sufficient in due course of time. Economic sectors like agriculture, industry and other service sectors are addressed through special policy measures so that there is all-round development of all the sectors of the economy. Service sectors such as transport, telecommunication and mass communication through radio and television services are given due importance in development. Through special area development programmes such as Drought Prone Area Programme, Command Area Development Programme, Wasteland Development Programme, Watershed Development Programme, Forest Development Programme and Tribal Area Development Programme, special emphasis is laid on the development of these regions.

Introduction of such schemes and the creation of special development authorities like the Western Orissa Development Council, Coastal Zone Development Authority, Chilka Development Authority, Orissa State Disaster Mitigation Authority, and administrative functionaries like KBK (Koraput, Bolangir, Kalahandi) Administrator and many development departments in the government to address specific issues of development, reflects the total commitment of the state government to all round development of the people and the state. However, in spite of all these schemes and the special development authorities and departments, the government is aware of the slow speed at which development efforts are actually reaching out to the target groups. It is also aware of the diversion of resources by intermediary functionaries and influential groups. This makes the schemes ineffective and erodes people's faith in the government's capability and sincerity. Therefore, the government is seized with the issues of how to bring about efficiency, effectiveness, accountability, transparency and reduce corruption in administration.

DEVELOPMENT STRATEGIES

The state government is always evolving new strategies to make the developmental schemes more and more effective. The first and foremost among the strategies is the creation and development of infrastructure that includes road, transport, telecommunication, post office, market, storage and collection centres, banks, electricity supply, agricultural service centres, *Krishi Vigyan Kendra*, public distribution centre, canal and other irrigation facilities, schools, hospitals, drinking water supply sources, etc. The range and quantity of infrastructure is increasing. However, the gap between the real need and what is available is still large. The distribution of infrastructure in various parts of the state is uneven. The government is generally aware of the poor maintenance of developmental infrastructure. Though the government is creating more and more such infrastructure over a period of time, up-to-date information on its total number, functional status and geographical distribution is lacking at the planning and decision-making levels.

Training and skills development are other aspects on which the government lays emphasis for making development schemes effective. Such training is required for government functionaries who are charged with the responsibility for implementing various development schemes. However, with the increasing number of schemes, the number of functionaries to be trained is very large. Thus, need for the training infrastructure is also very large.

Technology is a very important component of the strategy for making a development scheme effective. At times, technology provides a quantum leap to development. The high yielding varieties, sustained by higher doses of fertilisers and application of pesticides for plant protection have made the Green Revolution possible in India. Similar advances have been made in the fields of animal husbandry and fisheries. Recent advances have been made in plant breeding with genetic manipulation and the use of bio-fertilisers. Biological control of pests has resulted in substantial growth in agriculture and animal husbandry. Similar advances have been made in health care, especially in preventive medicine with the invention of vaccines and the rediscovery of herbal medicines. In the industrial sector, automation and new process technologies have made it possible to reach new heights of production and industrial safety. With people becoming more and more conscious of environmental pollution with respect to air, water and noise, new processes are demanded and brought is force through legislation and legal action.

Technology also helps in bringing objectivity to monitoring the implementation of development schemes and carrying out impact assessment. In this context, space imaging with a greater degree of clarity makes one time assessment of damage (crop loss due to drought, flood or cyclone, forest fire, damage to infrastructure due to earthquake and other natural or man-made calamities) and temporal monitoring of crop health, water bodies, watershed development programme, urbanisation, deforestation, etc. possible with greater accuracy and objectivity.

The state government is quite open to new ideas and new technology. It desires to adopt these as important components of government strategy for development whereas its realisation at the functional level meets with mixed responses. The government conceives of specific development schemes focused to achieve certain goals with respect to special sections of the society or economic sectors or regions. Accordingly, its implementation is given to special developmental functionaries. But, at the same time, the government is also aware that development schemes are interdependent in nature. Therefore, the government adopts the mission mode for implementation of some important development schemes such as Watershed Development Mission, Literacy Mission, Drinking Water Mission, etc. However, for other developmental schemes, this integration is achieved at the district level where the District Collector in his role as District Development Officer tries to coordinate with the district level officials of the line departments.

The government has realised that the active participation of the direct beneficiaries in project planning, scheduling project implementation and deciding the mode of implementation is very crucial for effective implementation of developmental schemes. Therefore, as a strategy, the government has been very consciously adopting a participatory approach to implementation of developmental schemes. Examples of such a participatory approach to implementation of development schemes are water users associations (*Pani Panchayat*), *Bhoomi Panchayat*, watershed association, *Vanasanrakshana Samiti*, *Palli Sabha*, *Gram Sabha*, etc. These grassroot level beneficiary groups meet regularly to discuss and decide issues, which otherwise could have created conflict and confrontation among them.

This is also a step towards achieving transparency in project implementation since there is a general distrust of the official machinery among people. However, in a large group, total participation is not achieved easily and decisions are generally biased in favour of opinion leaders. This is more so in a group which is ignorant of the schemes and the manner of their functioning.

Mass awareness is one of the strategies, which the government adopts for achieving transparency and accountability and for effective implementation of development schemes. Press and the electronic media like radio and television are used for this purpose. Besides, public meetings, distribution of leaflets and pamphlets on development schemes, street plays and folk dances in public places are also adopted. Displays of project details at public places like *panchayats* and block offices and on project sites or on the sides of roads are also made. However, the outreach of all such means is very limited. A good section of project functionaries at the field level are not fully aware of project details. Many government circulars on the matter are lost in the files and are not retrievable. However, the government realises that much more remains to be done to achieve its goals. Therefore, it continues its relentless effort by inventing newer strategies with the passage of time.

INITIATIVES TAKEN BY THE GOVERNMENT OF ORISSA UNDER THE GRAMSAT PILOT PROJECT

The government decides on developmental schemes and strategies for effective realisation of developmental goals. Various strategies are adopted by the government to achieve transparency and accountability, reduction of corruption and greater responsiveness.

The recent initiative taken by the government under the Gramsat Pilot Project addresses many aspects of governance, including issues of transparency, accountability, responsiveness, reduction of corruption, training and skills development, people's participation, project planning and monitoring, disaster warning, etc., besides providing live communication between the state capital, districts and blocks.

INFRASTRUCTURE FOR THE PROJECT AND ITS PROPOSED FUNCTIONING

VSAT and DRS Network

The Gramsat Pilot Project is a satellite based digital communication network. The space segment is supported by INSAT-3B in extended C-band. The ground segment of the network consists of a hub centre at Bhubaneswar, VSAT nodes at the district/block headquarters and DRS (Direct Reception System) nodes at *gram panchayats*.

Hub Centre at Bhubaneswar

The hub centre at Bhubaneswar will consist of a digital earth station providing satellite uplink. The VSAT hub will have hub electronics with a network manager and a series of server computers holding database and software. There will be a proxy server acting as a gateway to the Internet. The centre will also have a transmission studio to serve at the teaching end for interactive training and at the transmission end for broadcasting.

VSAT Nodes at 314 Blocks and 30 District Headquarters

At each of these 314 blocks and 30 district headquarters, there will be VSAT hardware consisting of VSAT outdoor unit and VSAT electronics with access router. There will be an Integrated Receiver and Decoder (IRD) and a television in a room with a seating capacity of 50–60 persons to serve as a classroom. The VSAT will have the capability to receive and transmit voice (phone), video (television/camera) and data (computer) simultaneously online between VSAT nodes and the hub centre. The VSAT, through an access router, will provide online computer connectivity from the VSAT base station at the block/district headquarters to a few offices in the block/ district towns using local telephone and modem. Each VSAT node will have a UPS with a battery, and a generator set for standby power backup in case of power failure. Though the Gramsat network proposes to provide this connectivity to 314 blocks and 30 district headquarters, the network is capable of supporting more VSAT nodes.

DRS Nodes at *Gram Panchayat* Headquarters

Under the Gramsat Pilot Project, it is proposed to provide Direct Reception Systems (DRS) to 800 *gram panchayats* in 8 KBK districts. Each DRS consists of a television, an integrated receiver and decoder (IRD) and an antenna. The television would be placed in the *gram panchayat* office where people can sit and watch programmes.

Through IRD, each of these nodes is capable of having a computer connected to the hub centre for transfer of data in broadcast mode. Although under the original project, it is proposed to provide 800 DRS to 800 *gram panchayats*, the network is capable of connecting unlimited number of DRS in broadcast mode.

DATABASE CREATION

Under the Gramsat Pilot Project, a master database will be created and made available in the network. This database would include spatial data on land information such as land use, landform, groundwater, geology, soils, slope, watershed, waterbody, village and forest boundaries, rail/road network, river and drainage network, canal network, telecommunication and power distribution network, rainfall, etc. A substantial part of this spatial information is derived from satellite images and this would be updated on a regular basis. The database would also have a complete layer of satellite data of various spatial resolution for the entire state. This would also be updated from time to time. Such data would be created on a 1:50,000 scale for the entire state and would be digitised in the the Geographic Information System, GIS. Besides, data on amenities and infrastructure (non-spatial but locational) such as markets, banks, cooperatives, industries, schools and colleges, health care centres, agro service centres, *Krishi Vigyan Kendras*, godowns, cold storages, collection centres, drinking water sources, lift irrigation points, irrigation wells, public distribution centres, post offices, telecom centres, bus stands, fertiliser depots, seed distribution centres, nursery, etc. for the entire state with location details would also be made available in the master database. Data on motor vehicles and boats as well as on road conditions and waterways will also be added. Data on demographic parameters and households would also form a part of this database. Household data will have elaborate details on each household and will form a vital component of the database. The government of Orissa is creating a digital database on Record of Rights (ROR). There is also a proposal to create a database for disaster mitigation, especially to address the issues of relief and rescue operation. The range of the database would keep expanding as and when it would be required to meet a special service need.

NETWORK APPLICATION

The Gramsat Pilot Project in Orissa will have five major applications:

1. Interactive training for skill development, technology transfer and dissemination of information.
2. Broadcasting of developmental information to people and to field functionaries at the grassroots level for achieving transparency and for encouraging participatory management in developmental schemes.
3. Access to spatial and non-spatial geographic information database for effective planning of development schemes, especially those relating to natural resources, environment and infrastructure development.
4. Management Information System for e-governance.
5. Disaster warning, relief and rescue operations and reconstruction.

Interactive Training for Skill Development, Technology Transfer and Dissemination of Information

The Gramsat Pilot Project at its hub centre at Bhubaneswar will have a studio which can serve as a teaching end. This studio is connected through the VSAT network to all the remote classrooms located at 30 district headquarters and 314 block headquarters for one-way video (through television) and two-way audio (through VSAT phone). Thus, any programme conducted in the studio can be received in audio and video through televisions in each of the remote classrooms. From the classrooms, questions can be raised through VSAT phones, which can be heard in the studio and transmitted back to all the remote classrooms such that a question raised in one remote classroom is heard in all the classrooms. This provides a virtual classroom situation connecting remote classrooms to the studio, which is the teaching end. Through such an arrangement, a large number of people can be trained through multimedia presentations at one time. The best of resource persons at the teaching end can interact directly with students in remote classrooms, and at the same time students in remote classrooms can have the benefit of viewing the best of teaching materials used by resource persons.

There is a critical need for the state government to impart training to its field functionaries on several aspects of developmental schemes. For example, in the case of watershed management, where the government issues guidelines from time to time, these can be discussed through interactive sessions wherein senior government officials can directly clarify issues to field functionaries. The government has taken up a large number of micro watersheds for development in the state. The number of such watersheds is nearly 2000 to 3000. The government has constituted a technical team for each block to provide guidance for watershed planning. This technical watershed development team consists of three to five members. Besides, there are project implementation agencies for each watershed. Thus, through interactive sessions with remote classrooms in 30 districts and 314 blocks, it is possible to interact with nearly 15,000 participants at any particular time. Similarly, a large number of *panchayati raj* functionaries, spread out all over the state, can be reached through this network for interaction by inviting them to assemble at their respective block headquarters. Similar is the case with departments like health and family welfare, women and child development, school and mass education where there is a need to impart training and interact with a large number of field level officials. It is also possible to have a quick review of projects/ schemes using the network. The higher officials of the state government can use the transmission end to interact with the field functionaries. The most important aspect of such interaction is the video recording of discussions, which can be preserved and reviewed in the future. A new kind of faith and confidence is instilled in the minds of field level functionaries when they see, hear and interact with higher officials using the network. Normally, the opportunity for face-to-face interaction comes to them very rarely, but through the network, it is possible to have such interactions frequently.

Apart from interactions and clarifications, the network can be used to improve technical skills with respect to any particular method that can be demonstrated on the network using a television camera. The processes and experiments can be demonstrated live by experts. For example, first aid treatment for sun stroke patients or simple aspects of repair and maintenance of handpumps can be demonstrated over the interactive network. Such interactive training is very effective when it comes to reaching out to a large number of persons at different locations and the training methods involved are simple. There will be substantial savings of time, money and efforts needed to mobilise the large number of persons to be trained, if the network is used for this purpose. There are more than 100,000 elected *panchayati raj* representatives and functionaries within the state. At present, there is no method by which they can be trained in their duties, responsibilities and functions within a reasonable period of time. However, it is now possible to train them through the Gramsat network within a few months.

At present, under the Gramsat Pilot Project in Orissa, interactive classrooms are effectively functioning in all the 30 district headquarters. About 50 interactive training sessions have been conducted. Many departments, viz. agriculture, health and family welfare, panchayati raj, energy, primary education, rural development, women and child development, forest and environment have conducted interactive training and all concerned government functionaries are more than happy about the outreach achieved. On the other hand, participants in remote areas are very excited at getting the opportunity to update their knowledge and to interact with top officials of the state government. Such programmes can be conducted by each department at least once a month.

Two reviews have been made—one by the Chief Secretary aided by very senior officials on the drought situation in western Orissa and the other by the High Court of Orissa on the functioning of Lok Adalats. A new programme, Operation Trishna, was launched through the network. This network can be used whenever there is new technology available and needs to be explained to all field functionaries for its widespread application in any project. Such interactive training sessions create a sense of participation and help in improvement of the skills of field level functionaries, which, in turn, would improve the transparency and effective implementation of developmental schemes.

Broadcasting of Developmental Information

The network under the Gramsat Pilot Project, has the capacity of connecting any number of direct reception systems. Therefore, it is possible to have direct reception systems in all *gram panchayats* or for that matter, in every village. In spite of the wide television networking, there are still large pockets in rural areas, which have no access to television. Further, the television network has become commercial in nature. Therefore, under the Gramsat network, the installed DRS are proposed to be used exclusively for developmental broadcasting. Such broadcasting will be particularly devoted to communicating messages on any development scheme, its functioning, the role of beneficiaries, contribution of the government and any other relevant details. Such information will encourage people's participation in various schemes as they would be aware of various aspects of the scheme.

Often, people are not fully aware of the benefits of the scheme. It is also observed that critical information is held back from people. In this context, it is necessary that the government communicate to the people directly, using the best of available mass media through this network. Such direct viewing by people is very effective, especially in a community where people are illiterate and have no access to the written media. At appropriate time, a video clipping of the statement by the chief minister or any high level government functionary would enhance credibility of the communication.

There are a large number of developmental schemes on which documentaries can be made. They can also be dramatised or artistically presented, appealing to people's emotions so that there is better reception and retention. Programmes can be made on a variety of social themes to dispel superstitions, highlighting the benefits of education, health care, environmental conservation and the nutritional value of locally available foodstuffs, especially vegetables and fruits. Special cultivation techniques, plant protection measures, animal husbandry, development of nursery, horticulture, drip and sprinkler irrigation can also be demonstrated through visual means to the people at large. The success stories of *Pani Panchayat, Bhumi Panchayat, Vanasamrakshan Samiti, Palli Sabha* can be replicated rapidly all over the state by showing programmes on them. Knowledge of new technology can spread almost instantly through this network. Programmes can be made keeping in mind the specific target groups and beneficiaries. An average broadcast of one hour every day can make an enormous impact on the people, thereby facilitating a great deal of transparency and peoples' participation.

Access to Spatial and Non-spatial Geographic information System Database

Under the Gramsat Pilot Project, a powerful database of spatial and non-spatial data covering the entire state will be created and the same will be made available in the network. Such a database will be derived from satellite remote sensing and other sources and it would be regularly updated. This database will make the process of planning very objective and technically sound. For example, the location of groundwater sources for irrigation or drinking water can be obtained from it. A settlement needing supply of drinking water or a stretch of land under agricultural or horticultural practices needing irrigation can be seen in the backdrop of potential ground water sites. Similarly, a patch of wasteland needing developmental interventions requires information on soil, slope, availability of water, which can be derived from the GIS database in the network and various development scenarios can be generated. Assessment of land suitability based on landform, landuse, soil, slope and other land and meteorological parameters taking information from the GIS database for the same area can be made for a variety of purposes. The GIS database can be used for infrastructure planning. For example, road alignment can be seen in the context of proximity to settlement, stability of the land with respect to slope, submergence of the route due to possible flooding based on the physiographic position, avoiding drainage to reduce the number of culverts and bridges, avoiding forest and agricultural lands and keeping off the wildlife sanctuaries. All such things are possible by referring to the spatial database in GIS.

Other infrastructure planning like establishment of schools, hospitals and godowns can be made keeping in view the service area and available road transport network. Such objective analysis of data can make decisions more rational. GIS database can present information on gap areas with respect to amenities and infrastructure, so that their distribution can be planned to equally benefit residents of all regions. Industrial planning can be more effective through a spatial analysis of markets, raw material, labour and the sources of water and power, besides the surrounding hinterland that has to support the industrial force with supplies of food, milk and vegetables. Thus, regional imbalance can be reduced through such spatial analysis of the database. Development schemes can be planned and their coverage decided through the spatial analysis of database. This would also help avoid undue political interference and make the decision making process more transparent.

Management Information System for E-governance

Under the Gramsat Pilot Project, the VSAT network will provide voice and data connectivity between block, district and the state capital. Communication through VSAT phones will be possible between block to block, block to district, block to state capital, district to block, district to district, district to state capital, and state capital to districts and blocks. At present, this VSAT voice communication may not look very exciting. However, at the time of any disaster due to flood or earthquake damaging the land connectivity, satellite based VSAT communication will provide meaningful backup. VSAT voice communication network being a close group communication network, would be more effective than the normal telecommunication network, as the latter has to support many other users on the network.

As regards online data connectivity through computers, it will be made available between block, district and the state capital. Connectivity to about eight offices each at the block and district towns and to almost all government offices in the state headquarters will be provided. It is also proposed to create a substantial database on schemes, infrastructure, households, demography and amenities. This database will cover all aspects of functioning of the government. Government departments and offices can access such online up-to-date information on the network through this connectivity, which will make the progress and impact monitoring of various schemes possible on a nearly real time basis.

Any query at the government level in the state capital, or any clarification at the field level by field functionaries can be instantly obtained through the network. Financial and physical reporting can be made very effective. Many public services can be delivered. For example, a nativity/residential certificate, or a ration card, or a driving licence, or a voter's identity card, or a caste or birth certificate, or a legal heir certificate can be applied for, prepared and delivered through the network since a household database and a record of rights database will be available in the network. This would make government and governance responsive. Online collection of entry tax and monitoring of movement of vehicles through check-posts can be done. Public distribution system can be made more effective, since the stock position and requirements of various outlets and godowns can be available on the network. Beneficiaries of welfare schemes such as below poverty line, and disabled and old age pension listing can be identified based on the household data in the network. This may eliminate bogus beneficiaries based on internal checks of the database. All tender information and sale of tender documents can be made through the network. Information on ongoing project works, their status and implementing agency can be put on the network for the information of the public so that there is widespread public awareness. Such details may include repair of roads, canals, construction of public buildings along with the cost and technical specifications.

It may be mentioned that it is possible to connect all DRS locations with a computer for data broadcast. On such computers, information of vital importance such as market rates of various commodities, agricultural practices, new government schemes or important public announcements can be put in the database and broadcast to computers connected to DRS locations, so that villagers and farmers at such places can avail the benefit of access to such information.

Disaster Warning, Relief and Rescue Operations and Reconstruction

Advance information on an impending disaster can be disseminated through this network to people in the affected area. With the spatial information in GIS available in the network, it would be possible to give precise information to people about the area of impact of any disaster. In the case of floods, with advance information on rainfall and water level in river systems, it is possible to know, through hydrological modeling, the area of possible submergence around a breach through the spatial database on contours and landforms. This, in turn, makes it possible to know which settlements and populations will be affected. The probable impact of such floods on road and other infrastructure, as well as on agricultural crops can also be known.

In the event of an actual disaster striking, be it a cyclone, flood, drought, or heat wave, one can know its area of impact through a spatial database integrated with real time satellite data. The extent of coverage and damage due to floods and drought can be assessed on a real time basis from space imagery giving details of the affected area and the population under its grip. Progressive mapping of a flood affected area can give clues about how to direct relief and rescue in the area. Such relief and rescue operations would also require database on necessary resources (vehicle for transport, boats for rescue operations, road clearing equipment) and supplies (food stock, drinking water, medicines, road construction materials, match box, kerosene, etc.) in the periphery of the affected areas from where it can be rushed to the affected site. It is also necessary to have a database on the workforce, which can be pressed into action during such trying times. It is necessary to ensure that the workforce, pressed into action, is from outside the affected zone, since the workforce in the affected area would not be in a proper frame of mind to offer its services.

CONCLUSION

The Gramsat Pilot Project is a unique experiment in the country. It encompasses development communication, upgradation of skills of government functionaries engaged in all areas, data connectivity, e-governance, disaster warning, and relief and rescue operations. Once the project, which is currently being implemented, is completed, it would be the largest VSAT network in the country. At present, only interactive training programmes for government functionaries are being conducted by installing a fly away terminal (given by ISRO) in a studio at Cuttack. So far, such interactive training programmes have generated a lot of interest and enthusiasm amongst government functionaries of various departments. This has led to increasing demand for the network from government departments. Taking into consideration the initial response of government functionaries and various departments to the network, there can be little doubt that the Gramsat Pilot Project will be a major success story.

13

E-governance for Improved Service: Choices Made by Tamil Nadu

— M. Anandakrishnan

INTRODUCTION

Information technology (IT) is of greater advantage to countries having traditional modes of working. The high degree of alienation between the citizens and administrators can also be reduced through IT. The needless harassment experienced by people, especially those with low levels of literacy, either due to the indifference of the administrative staff or exploitation by middlemen, can be eliminated. E-governance should involve the beneficiaries and administrators at various levels in the implementation of programmes and in service delivery. Top-down solutions, no matter how elegant and sophisticated they may be, are unlikely to be sustained at the grassroots level. The incorporation of e-governance requires patience and understanding. Given the technological capabilities, there will be temptation to institute e-governance solutions to a wide-ranging array of administrative tasks. Prudence, however, should dictate the choice of priority tasks and a clear definition of objectives for e-governance.

OBJECTIVES OF IT IN ADMINISTRATION

Almost any administrative function can be computerised. But computerisation in itself will solve nothing unless the objective is properly stated and sought to be achieved with deliberate action. The following should be the objectives of IT in administration:

1. Deliver essential services to citizens.

2. Enhance productivity and efficiency of administrative functions.
3. Eliminate touts and undesirable practices such as speed money, delays, harassment and unnecessary documents.
4. Impart a citizen-friendly image to the government.
5. Ensure transparency and right to information in governmental activities.
6. Establish a database for decision-making including forecasting.
7. Maintain control over assets, revenue and expenditure.
8. Encourage public awareness and participation in key areas of developmental efforts.

APPLICATIONS OF E-GOVERNANCE

E-governance can help in rendering various services. We shall now discuss these services.

Services for Citizens

Among the various e-governance services, the ones that deserve highest priority are those intended to benefit vast populations, which would otherwise face serious hardships for getting essential services. Depending on the volume of demand for citizens' services and the availability of resources, the government will have to determine the phases in which they are to be implemented. The population groups to be covered by new services and the specific list of services to be implemented will have to be planned in stages. Kerala has identified *panchayats* as the basic unit and has prepared a list of services to be delivered in all its *panchayats*. Tamil Nadu has chosen *taluks* as the basic unit and has started implementation of a list of services to be available in all the 206 *taluks* of the state. Some of these services are also made available at the level of 102 municipalities and 6 corporations of the state. Though these services may start off as stand-alone localised functions, steps would have to be taken to create data storage systems and network communication facilities to make them available extensively, with speed and reliability.

The reservation system currently made available by the Indian Railways is an excellent example of a citizens' service wherein the uncertainties and harassment experienced in matters of reservation and booking has been eliminated. However, the proprietary nature of the software used in e-governance may involve high financial strains, thereby reducing the capacity to expand the services. Hence, some initial thought should be devoted to the possibility of adopting open-source based software which can adequately perform the desired functions. Another issue, which needs attention, is the use of local languages in creating data systems and in delivery of services. The services should not be limited to English only. Fortunately, there is a high level of competency in the country to overcome the constraints of proprietary software and also to develop multilingual software in Indian languages. These two attributes should be central to the design of e-governance systems and should be standardised in a manner that the transportability of data and information should be possible without encumbrances.

There are various services, which can be rendered to the citizens through e-governance.

Entitled Services

Citizens are entitled to certain services from the state and they should be able to obtain them easily on request. It is common experience that citizens are subjected to unnecessary harassment due to corruption at lower levels and exploitation by middlemen, to avail services meant for them. Besides providing the necessary hardware and software, it is essential to provide sufficiently trained and helpful staff. This should be followed by supervision by senior officials, adequate dissemination of information to the people and a grievance redressal system.

Tamil Nadu has completed the installation of computers in all the 206 *taluks* and 102 municipalities and 6 corporations. Software have been installed at all the *taluks* and most of the local bodies enabling them to render this category of entitled services, relating to the issue of birth, death, income, solvency, legal heir and community certificates. Each unit has set time limits ranging from three to seven days for the issue of these certificates. The municipalities and corporations are also equipped to issue birth and death certificates. In addition, the *taluk* level facility contains the software for issue of certificates relating to *patta* transfers and *patta* classification. This has become possible because of the advance preparations during the last three or four years in Tamil Nadu to fully computerise all land records from the 'A' registers and the *chittas*. The software also includes features relating to land assignment, acquisition, relinquishment, alienation, encroachment, settlement and revenue. An additional welcome feature at the *taluk* level is the computerisation of old-age pension details pertaining to the particular area. The software for all these functions was developed and installed by the National Informatics Centre (NIC). The NIC also provides necessary technical training to the operating staff and assists in maintaining and upgrading the software for specific local needs.

Welfare Services

There are many services offered as privileges to specific groups of citizens. Concessionary loans, special grants and subsidies of various kinds fall under this category. Those who are eligible for such benefits should be able to obtain them expeditiously. Through computer-based service, it should be possible to substantially improve the service delivery. The list of such services implemented in Tamil Nadu at the *taluk* level includes scholarships, welfare payments to the aged and the handicapped, widows and destitute women, and agricultural labourers and students.

Grievance Redressal

Citizens should be properly guided to register their grievances and be assured of satisfactory measures for redressal. A system which offers an easy outlet for their agony and enables serious consideration of their problems will enhance the citizens' respect for the administration. This will also provide an opportunity to the government for assessment of people's problems and encourage official accountability.

Public Information

Citizens should have access to information related to various policies, procedures, development schemes, government orders and official pronouncements on matters concerning their life and work. Such information is particularly valuable to people living far from cities and towns and do not have an easy access to information. Providing such information in the local language is the government's duty as it recognizes its citizens right to information. Access to such information by the citizens will depend upon the availability of well-connected information centres. The *panchayat* or *taluk*, or block or district level computer centres can offer such information services as add-on facilities. Local schools and colleges having computer facilities could also offer this service as a matter of public interest. Community based Internet centres for public information and communication can also be set up.

Community Internet Centres

Tamil Nadu's scheme of Community Internet Centres (CIC) envisages the establishment of a large number of such centres with the active involvement of the government, voluntary organisations and private enterprises. Since a large proportion of the population in India, especially in rural areas, cannot afford to own computers and Internet connection, the CICs offer them the facility to use the Internet for getting useful information at an affordable cost.

The CICs will render multifunctional services to the population in their area.

They would focus primarily on enabling the local population to use e-mail facilities in English and the local language to seek and obtain essential market-related information about commodity prices and agricultural inputs. The range of services also include rapid information about medical and educational facilities according to the student's specific interest and need, to procure printouts of various application forms for different services offered by the government departments, educational institutions, financial institutions, scholarship schemes, etc., and other information on areas of interest related to local, state, national or international events.

In establishing the CICs, all possible technological options are being explored to provide essential connectivity and adequate bandwidth to meet the requirements of the 'last mile' problems. For communities situated in far-flung areas, the Wireless in Local Loop (WiLL) source linked to local exchanges is economical and technically feasible. For some locations, cable connection or optic fibre connection may be convenient.

Managing Assets and Liabilities

Every governmental organisation possesses assets. These vary in form, value, durability and usage. They are either movable, immovable or consummable. It is in the interest of the organisation to document the status of their assets for preventing their pilferage and misuse as well as for auditing and public trust. In case of assets that are frequently used and replenished, proper documentation helps to maintain inventory levels consistent with demand, thereby avoiding dead investments. Private corporations have realised the economic value of documenting their assets using Information Technology, to enable quick reviews and appraisal.

Most agencies possess movable and immovable assets, which are of considerable value. Some of them are in the form of real estates generating revenue. Details of their locations, value, assignment, rentals, maintenance, disposal, etc. are often maintained in scattered registers that could be organised in a manner facilitating their proper management and deployment, by use of computerised and networked databases.

Collection of revenue can be enhanced by developing e-governance procedures. This will also help a great deal in budgeting, financial accounting and management. Bank deposits, payment liabilities and loans can be streamlined to introduce a high degree of efficiency. The tendering process for new acquisitions and various disposals and services can be made transparent and reliable. Considerable progress has been made by the municipalities and corporations of Tamil Nadu in incorporating asset management software for functions related to the collection of property tax, water charges, profession tax, licencing, lease-rentals, vehicle maintenance, etc.

Department Specific Functions

Some of the departments have substantial public interaction. Some have major regulatory responsibilities. The jurisdiction of some is limited, while others may be widely distributed. The creation and maintenance of large database and effective networking between these departments is thereby required.

In Tamil Nadu, the departments which have taken such initiatives include revenue, commercial taxes, registration, transport, municipal administration and water supply, electricity board, civil supplies and public distribution system, medical services, prohibition and excise, police, rural development, industries, school education, higher education, and public works. Each department has hosted the information on its website or on the State Government website in English and Tamil.

Internal Administrative Function

Use of archaic filing system and registers, stock rooms, and hassles in knowing and locating what is available on record are generally the reasons for the administration's poor image. Notes, recommendations and decisions should be computerised. In a bid to make the government function efficiently, file monitoring system, payroll accounts, leave-related information, financial management, personnel information system, provident fund accounts and audit objections are being computerised in Tamil Nadu.

Planning and Forecasting Function

Various tools, techniques and computer software like GIS are used for the collection, storage dissemination and analysis of data for planning. Another e-governance tool available for planning is the data warehousing system. A massive volume of data is generated in course of the state's governmental activities. Such data remain with different offices in the form of registers, files and reports. Data warehousing helps to collect, collate, store and retrieve data in an organised manner. The Tamil Nadu government, with the help of NIC, has taken steps to establish an Internet based data warehousing system from April 2001.

CONCLUSION

Significant advances will be made with the availability of trained personnel and the development of IT infrastructure in the country. Some IT initiatives which will enable e-governance are yet to be taken. There is a need to properly identify the functions where IT can be applied. Likewise, there is also need for proper devolution of responsibilities and development of broad guidelines and framework for enabling implementation at different levels. There has to be focus on monitoring the implementation of the IT policy, development of skills and attitudes for IT and adequate provision of financial and human resources.

IT led governance has changed the way the administration functions in Tamil Nadu. The services to be given to the people, the management of assets and liabilities, functions of various departments, and planning and monitoring system have been made fast and easy with the application of IT. With an effective IT policy, orientation and training of employees, awareness citizen's about IT and adequate budgetary provisions, e-governance holds much in store for the nation and its states.

14

Perspectives on Democratic Decentralised Governance for Rural Development in Mizoram

— R.N. Prasad
— Lalneihzovi

INTRODUCTION

Democracy, as a form of government, signifies the empowerment of people and grassroots democracy ensures genuine participatory development process at the local level. A grassroots democracy, in other words, is essentially decentralised democracy in which the management of public affairs does not begin and end at the top, but operates through a wide network of people's participating units in local areas. Hence, these become real centres of power, democratic thought and action. However, it is necessary to consider the fundamental differences between a local government and a local self-government. A local government, which is an agent of the central or the state government, performs only the agency role and functions, and so it does not enjoy decision-making power and financial autonomy. A local self-government means a democratic, decentralised government in the sense that it is elected and responsive to the felt needs of the people of a limited geographical area and endowed with autonomy—legal, political, administrative, functional and financial. Thus, it enjoys the powers of decision-making on all matters within its functional geographical area and remains accountable to the local people for the exercise of powers and functions and the use of public funds devolved upon it. However, units of local self-government do not enjoy adequate powers to function effectively. Hence, adequate political, administrative, economic and financial powers have to be devolved to the units to enable them to discharge their functions and responsibilities effectively.

This chapter briefly discusses the importance of democratic decentralisation with reference to the *panchayati raj* and the 73rd Constitutional Amendment Act, 1992. Further, it discusses democratic decentralisation in the state of Mizoram. It will examine how the 73rd Amendment, 1992 will achieve grassroots democratic polity by making *panchayati raj* an instrument of local self-government. A comparative study of the local units of Autonomous District Councils and Village Councils existing in Mizoram with the *panchayati raj* is also attempted. Lastly, it is important to synthesise the positive thrusts of Village Councils, Autonomous District Councils and the 73rd Constitutional Amendment, 1992.

DEMOCRATIC DECENTRALISATION

Decentralisation means the transfer of authority by delegation to field level, or by devolution to local authorities or local bodies. It is specifically the transfer of authority—judicial or administrative from a higher level of government to a lower level. Further, decentralisation is a method embracing both processes of de-concentration and devolution. De-concentration stands for the delegation of authority adequate for the discharge of specific functions to a staff of a central department which is situated outside the headquarters, while devolution is the legal conferring of powers to discharge specified or residual functions upon formally constituted local authority. In the organisational context, it refers to delegation of decision-making.

Decentralisation, thus, symbolises democratic values. It is a process of power-sharing in decision-making and is based on the principle that most decisions are taken by the people, who are affected by them. Decentralisation of power aims at better and faster communication, involvement and commitment of the people in development, mobilisation of support and utilisation of resources in a better manner for national development, reduction in delay in decision-making, greater equity in allocation of resources and investments as well as reduction in apathy of administration towards clientele. But the institutional machinery of democratic decentralisation should be elective. Decentralised authority should not become the monopoly of an individual, but should be vested in a committee. Democratic decentralisation is a necessary precondition for socio-cultural and politico-economic development, as greater equity is presumed more likely when representatives from various walks of life take part in deciding developmental issues. Any form of community development without decentralised democracy will be ineffective. Hence, the grassroots institutions are crucial for democratic, decentralised governance for rural development.

After Independence, rural development has been one of the constant goals of the five-year plans. It forms the crux of India's developmental strategy. Rural development programmes aim at the improvement of the living standards of the rural poor by providing them opportunities for the fullest utilisation of their potential through active participation in the process of goal-oriented change. They also enable the use of human and natural resources in rural areas and reduce area-wise disparities. In order to achieve the goals of rural upliftment, the district administrative machinery has been restructured/democratised, to ensure an efficient utilisation of rural resources for purposes of development and a more equitable share of development benefits to the rural poor.

Development programmes have a better chance of success, legitimacy, equity and effectiveness when the target group and the general public participate in the various steps of the developmental decision-making process viz., planning, implementing, monitoring and evaluation of development policies and schemes and sharing fruits of development. Democratic participation is, thus, a community venture, and only when this process is recognised, will it attain its full potential. In fact, the essence of democracy is the participation of all citizens making decisions that affect them.

Decentralisation is a prime mechanism through which democracy becomes truly representative and responsive. With transfer of development functions and vesting of necessary powers, the *panchayati raj* will be better able to undertake development programmes. The following are the aims of the *panchayati raj*:

1. Providing a broad base to democracy by striving to achieve the cherished ideal of village self-government.
2. Affording the much needed training ground for future leadership.
3. Creating awareness and initiative in the rural people about community development programmes.
4. Proper utilisation of the available manpower and other rural resources which have remained mostly under exploited and unutilised.
5. Developing a sense of community feeling and self reliance in the villagers.
6. Helping the weaker sections of the community to participate in the management of rural affairs.
7. Improving rural consciousness among the officials and impressing upon them the utility of coordinated and inter-related approach to various development programmes.
8. Ensuring quicker acceptance of new ideas in the countryside.
9. Planning a balanced, overall development of the rural areas, thereby raising the standards of living of the rural people.

The provision for the *panchayati raj*, as a framework of rural local self-government with inbuilt decentralising tendencies, was incorporated in the non-justiciable Directive Principles of State Policy (Part IV) of the Constitution of India. Article 40, which is a directive to the states stipulates, 'the states shall take steps to organise village *panchayats* and endow them with such power and authority as may be necessary to enable them to function as units of self government'. Thus, the *panchayati raj* is an institution placed at different levels to accomplish the multiple goals and tasks of the rural local self-governments.

The 73rd Amendment, 1992

In order to improve the participation of rural people in the process of their development, and involvement in decision-making, and decentralised planning directly affecting their lives, the Government of India has provided constitutional status to village *panchayats* under the 73rd Amendment, 1992. It envisages grassroots democratic polity by making *panchayati raj* an instrument of local self-government and community development. The Act provides reservation for women and weaker sections to ensure their participation at all levels of the *panchayati raj* institutions (PRIs). It has brought constitutional status and uniformity to PRIs by making the three-tier system a permanent feature. It has regularised the electoral process by making elections imperative after every five years at the completion of term of the PRIs. Elections will be conducted under the supervision of the State Election Commission. The provision for setting up state finance commissions guarantees financial autonomy/financial devolution to the PRIs. A district planning committee is to be constituted to consolidate the plans prepared by the *panchayats*. The PRIs are also made accountable for the maintenance and audit of their accounts. As regards functional devolution, specific legal transfer of powers and responsibilities has been made to the PRIs to prepare plans for economic development and social justice, including any matter listed in the Eleventh schedule (29 subjects). Thus, enough care has been taken to make the *gram panchayats* effective institutions of grassroots democracy to ensure genuine participatory development process at the village level. The Act aims at reducing political and bureaucratic interference in rural development programmes. Briefly, it can be said that India is on the threshold of a historic transition of political power to the grassroots with all states having completed the process of enacting fresh legislation on April 23, 1994 to strengthen the PRIs. But mere legislative enactment does not ensure effectiveness and viability of the PRIs in the states. What is more important is their operationalisation. It is the political will of the state governments that is the most important pre-condition for the successful functioning of the PRIs.

We will be dealing with the democratic decentralisation in Mizoram and making a comparative study of the existing systems of the local government with the *panchayati raj* system.

LOCAL GOVERNMENT IN MIZORAM

After Independence, a new scheme of simple and inexpensive administration for the tribesmen of certain hill districts of the then state of Assam, based on the recommendations of the Bardoloi Sub-Committee, the North-East Frontier Tribal and Excluded Areas Sub-Committee of the Constituent Assembly, was incorporated in the Sixth Schedule of the Constitution of India. This provided for the constitution of the Autonomous District Councils (ADCs) for major tribesmen and Autonomous Regional Councils for minor tribesmen other than the major tribal people within a district. As a result, the Autonomous Mizo Hills Districts Council for the Mizos and the Pawi-Lakher Regional Council (PLRC) for the Pawi, Lakher and Chakma tribes were set up in 1952 and 1953 respectively. Both the councils democratised village administration by enacting the Lushai Hills District (Village Councils) Act, 1953 and the Pawi Lakher Autonomous Region (Village Councils) Act, 1954 under sub-clause (e) of clause (3) of the Sixth Schedule of the Constitution of India. Accordingly, the village administration was vested in the democratically elected village councils (VCs), which started functioning from August, 1954 within the respective jurisdictions of the councils. The village councils have very limited functions and mostly administrative and judicial powers of a petty nature under the Village Councils' Act of 1953 and 1954. When the Mizo Hills District was elevated to the status of the Union Territory of Mizoram in accordance with the North-Eastern Areas (Reorganisation) Act, 1971, the Autonomous Mizo Hills District Council was abolished in 1972. The Pawi–Lakher Regional Council was trifurcated into three district councils, viz. the Lai District Council, the Mara District Council and the Chakma District Council under the provision of the said Act. The Lushai Hills District (Village Councils) Act, 1953 and the Pawi–Lakher Regional Council (Village Councils) Act, 1954 have been adopted by the Government of Mizoram and the three Autonomous District Councils as well, since 1972 for the administration of village affairs in their respective areas. The provisions of the Acts can be amended by executive/ administrative orders of the government and the Autonomous District Councils. Briefly, Mizoram has two sets of the Village Councils over which the Government of Mizoram and the District Councils extend their jurisdictions independently.

DEMOCRATIC DECENTRALISATION IN MIZORAM

Article 243 M of the Constitution relating to *panchayats* is not applicable to Mizoram mainly due to the operation of the democratically elected village councils since 1954. Though, the Government of Mizoram is concerned with the implementation of the provisions of part IX of the Constitution in the state, no positive steps have been taken so far to implement the constitutional provisions relating to the *panchayats* to ensure empowerment of the state's rural tribesmen and their participation in the decision-making and implementing processes. This, no doubt, contradicts the principle of democratic decentralised governance for rural development, as well as the provisions of the Directive Principles of the State Policy of the Indian Constitution. The essential prerequisites for the *panchayati raj* to function effectively as an institution of self-government is to have clearly demarcated operational areas, adequate power and authority commensurate with responsibilities, necessary human and financial resources, functional autonomy and non-interference from outside agencies. The new *panchayats* will have administrative, financial and political powers contributing towards strengthening the planning process at the micro level and will look into overall rural development and improvement of access to decision-making bodies by the poor. These have been mentioned in 29 operative subjects incorporated in the Eleventh Schedule (Article 243-G) of the Constitution (73rd Amendment, 1992). These subjects include creation and maintenance of social services and productive infrastructure in rural areas, and promotion of productive development activities and social service programmes. Briefly, the *panchayats* have larger scope to accelerate socio-economic development in rural areas as compared to the Autonomous District Councils and Village Councils existing in the state.

The Village Councils are created by an enactment of the Government of Mizoram and the Autonomous District Councils and their provisions are amended by executive/administrative orders. The *panchayats*, on the other hand, are created by the Constitution of India, and thereby have constitutional status. The Village Councils are single-tier rural administrative institutions without the status of rural local self-governing bodies. The 73rd Constitutional Amendment, 1992 ensures holding of elections to the *panchayats* within six months of their dissolution. In the case of Village Councils, this is not mandatory. These councils have been denied the devolution of financial resources, administrative responsibilities, political powers, development roles, planning, decision-making and implementing processes. Thus, the councils lack political, functional and financial powers. Socio-economic development of the poor rural tribesmen is beyond the scope of the Village Councils which have neither created significant impact at the village level nor have provided leadership to the local community due to lack of financial, political and development powers. The Village Council provides for women to contest elections but does not provide for the reservation of seats for them. So women cannot participate in grassroots democracy. It only provides judicial and administrative powers/responsibilities to male tribesmen. The new *panchayats* stipulate/ensure the reservation of one-third of the elected seats and posts of chairpersons for the women of scheduled castes/scheduled tribes/other backward castes at all three levels, viz. village, block and district. *Panchayats*, thus, ensure women's participation in the decision-making and implementing processes. Briefly, the Village Councils have failed to evoke local initiative and people's participation in development activities and in bringing about social and economic changes in the rural areas owing to the strong centralising tendency in the state. Such a process of centralisation is not compatible with the spirit of decentralisation. A question arises whether the Village Councils are worthy enough to be equated with self-governing institutions.

From the foregoing it appears that both the Village Councils and the *panchayats* differ structurally and operationally. However, the Constitutional Amendment Act, 1992 fall's short in some respects such as the devolution of judicial function. The Village Councils have judicial functions, whereas, the 73rd Amendment does not stipulate devolution of judicial powers to the *gram panchayats*. So the provisions of Part IX of the Constitution need to be amended. The judicial functions carried out by the Village Councils should also be entrusted to the *gram panchayats*.

The Autonomous District Councils also lack adequate powers. These councils focus entirely on the district as there are no democratic tiers below the district. Moreover, the dissolution of the Autonomous District Councils is not accompanied by mandatory reconstitution. The Sixth Schedule does not provide for holding elections within six months after dissolution, as in Part IX of the Constitution. All receipts/money of the Autonomous District Councils are credited to the Consolidated Fund of the State. So it totally depends on the state government for its funds/finances. The state government controls its finances and expenditures. It does not have financial autonomy. Lack of financial autonomy takes away the autonomous character of the District Councils. No real autonomy has been conferred on them.

The Autonomous District Councils have no mandatory development or welfare functions. They take up such development activities and social services as are assigned by the state government. But these functions depend very much on the political parties, which run the state administration. If the same political party is in power both at the state and at the district levels, the latter's programme of developmental activities will be smooth sailing. It thus seems that the Autonomous District Councils enjoy less power in some cases and in some other cases, they are so hedged by the political whims of the state level political elite that their effective functioning becomes problematic.

What is required is that members of the legislature should cut across party lines and implement the new system of *panchayats* with suitable nomenclature and terminology that is familiar to the tribesmen. This should be done in true spirit, with the implicit purpose of empowering the rural people and plugging the loopholes and shortcomings of the existing system. The state government should enact the necessary laws to incorporate the provisions of the 73rd Amendment Act, 1992.

CONCLUSION

The 73rd Constitutional Amendment provides for institutions of self-government at the district, block and village levels and regular elections to them. Fairness of elections is ensured through the setting up of a State Election Commission. It also gives substantial financial powers to levy, collect and appropriate taxes, duties, tolls and fees. It also provides for mandatory setting up of the State Finance Commission for proper devolution of financial resources. The Consolidated Fund of India, under the first provision to Article 275(1) meant specifically for promotion of welfare and administration of Scheduled Areas can transfer additional resources to tribal areas. Money gets credited to the fund of the *panchayats* at different tiers. It mandates *panchayats* to prepare plans for economic development and social justice. The Act provides for devolution of 29 subjects to *panchayats*. It also reserves not less than one third of seats and positions for women. There is reservation of SCs/STs in proportion of their population to the total population. Briefly, this Act seeks to enshrine democracy at the grassroots. It also intends to give power to the people. Thus, the greater the power of the *panchayats*, the better it is for the people. It will end corruption and eliminate power-brokers and middlemen from politics.

It is suggested that the application of the provisions of Part IX of the Constitution by the state and the Sixth Scheduled Areas to their respective jurisdictions appears to be necessary. While retaining the Autonomous District Councils in these areas, additional advantages like devolution of powers, functions, financial benefits and reservation of seats, etc. granted by the 73rd Constitutional Amendment should be extended to them, as well as to lower bodies, as recommended by the regional and sub-regional workshops on *panchayats* sponsored by the Rajiv Gandhi Foundation for north-eastern states. While accepting the system of *panchayati raj*, there should be no fear that the powers of the autonomous district councils would be curtailed once the *panchayats* are constituted. Undoubtedly, their authoritative superiority would remain intact. Just like the central and state governments, the district councils and *panchayats* are two separate, independent bodies and they cannot be linked without a Constitutional amendment. It is left to the Union Legislature (Parliament) and the state legislature to make necessary laws on the *panchayats* and District Councils respectively. As regards the application of the constitutional provisions to the Sixth Scheduled Areas, it is better to agree with L.S. Gassah, who has aptly said that if the *panchayati raj* bodies under the 73rd Constitutional Amendment are not introduced in the Sixth Schedule Areas, these areas will enjoy less powers of self-government (in development aspect) than the rest of the country. The 73rd Amendment provides more autonomy to the local bodies. But since the Sixth Schedule has a long history of tribal struggle for assertion of ethnic identity, it cannot be dispensed with easily. Therefore, to synthesise the positive thrust of both, a system, as already suggested by the workshops on *panchayats* in the region, will have to be evolved. It may further be added that the Bhuria Committee, 1995, also felt and recommended that while certain provisions of the 73rd Amendment were wholesome and should be incorporated in the law to be passed by Parliament under Article 43-M (4) (b), certain unique characteristics of tribal societies and tribal areas need to be kept in view.

REFERENCES

1. Bava, Noorjahan, 'Resource mobilization for PRIs: tax assignments and tax transfers', *Souvenir of Indian Institute of Public Administration*, Delhi Regional Branch, August, 1998.
2. Prasad, R.N., *Public Administration in North-East India*, Vikas Publishing House, New Delhi, 1998, p. 66.
3. Prasad, R.N. and A.K. Agarwal, *Political and Economic Development of Mizoram*, Mittal Publications, New Delhi,1991, pp. 113–117.
4. Prasad, R.N., *Mizoram and the Constitution (Seventy Third Amendment) Act, 1992, relating to Panchayats*, (This paper was presented at the national seminar on 'Panchayats', organised by the Rajiv Gandhi Foundation, New Delhi, on 22–23 December, 1997) (Unpublished).
5. Karna, M.N., L.S. Gassah and C.J. Thomas (Eds.), *Power to People in Meghalaya*, Regency Publications, New Delhi, 1998, pp. 160–161.

15

Lessons in Organising Self Help: A Case Study of the Sukhomajri Water Resources Management Project

— Ramanjit Kaur Johal

INTRODUCTION

A long held view that people do not want to contribute to better their lives has been disproved by the villagers of Sukhomajri, located in the foothills of the Shivaliks in the Panchkula district of Haryana. The World Bank, has not only confirmed it, but on its strength shown an inclination to fund such projects in India. This chapter deals with how a self-help group in the village contributed to better people's lives through participatory natural resource management.

There are many success stories of people's initiatives that fall broadly within the framework of self-help groups. Interestingly, the predominant areas of their operations are natural resource management and micro-credit finance. However, few mass movements have precipitated inspite of these success stories. The Ninth Five Year Plan recognises that the initiatives of NGOs are rich and diverse and that these efforts have often demonstrated the success of alternative models of development. It calls upon the NGOs to organise women into self-help groups for initiating the process of empowerment.

The case selected for this chapter is a success story of participatory natural resource management—The Sukhomajri Watershed Management Project. Its success has spawned a host of similar projects in the region. Data and information has been collected from both secondary and primary sources.

SUKHOMAJRI WATERSHED MANAGEMENT PROJECT

Sukhomajri is a small hamlet of about 100 families with an average land holding of 0.57 hectares. It is located in the foothills of the Shivaliks at a distance of about 30 kilometres northeast of Chandigarh.

Until 1975, Sukhomajri had no source of regular irrigation. Its entire agricultural land (52 hectares) was under rain-fed single cropping. Small land holdings, coupled with frequent crop failures due to erratic rainfall made agriculture the least dependable means of livelihood. Consequently, the people of Sukhomajri turned to animal husbandry. But, once the domestic animals, especially goats and cows, were allowed to graze freely in the nearby hills, followed by indiscriminate felling of trees for fuel and other domestic uses, the result was a complete denudation of the hill slopes for several kilometers around. Further, the seasonal torrential rains resulted in uncontrolled rainwater from about 4.2 hectares of denuded hilly catchments converting the nearby agricultural fields into about 20 metre deep and wide gullies.

In 1975, the continuing problem of silting of the prestigious man-made Sukhna lake in Chandigarh drew the attention of the Central Soil and Water Conservation Research and Training Institute, Research Centre, Chandigarh. Their reconnaissance survey revealed that the major source of the sediment was the catchment area located in close proximity of Sukhomajri and a few nearby villages. The denuded hill slopes caused sedimentation.

The Research Centre, Chandigarh submitted a project proposal for sediment control in Sukhna lake to the Indian Council for Agricultural Research. It was indeed fortunate that the US Ford Foundation had, at that juncture, set aside funds especially for funding watershed management projects. The Sukhomajri proposal fitted the bill, resulting in a $40,000 grant in 1975. In the vicinity of Sukhomajri, the research centre identified about 85 acres of badly eroded topmost catchment area responsible for silting the lake. The area was subjected to two-fold treatment: one included mechanical/structural measures and the other included massive vegetative measures. However, neither met with success in the absence of cooperation from the people of Sukhomajri. Though silting was of prime concern to the research centre, the same was insignificant to the people of Sukhomajri.

It was only with the help of local people that a ray of hope emerged. The research centre gave credit to the village elders, Jethu Ram and Daulat Ram, who showed them the way. Thus, with hints from the village elders, it was realised that no amount of scientific and technical anti-erosion measures would succeed unless the people of Sukhomajri were provided with an alternative source of livelihood.

With technology created by the research centre, four earthen dams were built between 1976 and 1985. Funds from the Ford Foundation helped in providing gainful employment to the villagers involved in the construction of these dams. These dams serve the following three main purposes:

1. The dams instantly check the gully formation in agricultural fields and thereby effectively prevent silting through the erosion of soil.
2. They store surplus rainwater from the catchment area, to be used for irrigation after the withdrawal of the monsoon.
3. The dams enable rehabilitation of the catchments.

EMERGENCE OF THE CONCEPT OF SOCIAL FENCING

The most apparent and instant benefit was in the form of manifold increase in agricultural production due to the availability of water for irrigation. This made the people of Sukhomajri realise the value of protection of vegetation in the catchments. Then it was not difficult for them to perceive that the protection of forests was the protection of their own interests. This is what came to be termed *social fencing.* It means that the society will protect the hilly watersheds from grazing and illicit cutting of vegetation. The forest areas, which wore a desolate look at the beginning of the project, were covered with grass and trees within a period of 10–15 years.

CHANGE IN CATTLE COMPOSITION

Social compulsions, economic considerations, self-restraint and the availability of ample fodder, both from forest area and agricultural fields, brought about a dramatic change in the cattle composition in the village. A filip was given to the dairy sector and milk production increased substantially over the years as is apparent from Table I.

TABLE 15.1 Number of Milch Cattle and Milk Yield (Litres/day) 1975–2000

Milch Cattle	*1975*	*1981*	*1985*	*1992*	*2000*
Buffaloes	79	148	149	221	257
Cows	14	6	6	9	13
Goats	246	36	8	37	45
Milk Yield	248	658	670	995	1018

Source: Central Soil and Water Conservation Training Institute, Research Centre, Chandigarh.

CONSTITUTION OF A VILLAGE SOCIETY

A village society was constituted in 1979 following discussions between the Research Centre's representatives and the villagers. It was agreed that the entire management of the project should be handed over to the society. Initially it was called "Water Users' Association", and renamed later as Hill

Resources Management Society (HRMS) registered under the Society's Registration Act, 1860. The head of every family, whether owning land or not, was entitled to membership. This gave rise to the concept of sharing responsibilities and benefits on the basis of equity. The society performs the following three functions: (i) protection of hilly areas from grazing and illicit felling of trees; (ii) distribution of irrigation water from dams on payment basis; and (iii) maintenance of dams, water conveyance systems and other assets.

The society's income comes from irrigation water charges, sale of *bhabbar* (raw grass) and fodder grass from the forest area, income from leasing dam for fish culture, fines imposed and membership fee. The profits are used by HRMS for welfare activities like the maintenance of dams and irrigation conveyance systems in the village. During 1999–2000, the society purchased a 350 sq. yards plot of land for setting up a village community centre.

ELIMINATION OF FOREST CONTRACTOR

The forest area close to Sukhomajri was originally leased to private contractors by the Haryana Forest Department for extraction of fodder and *bhabbar* grass used as a raw material for paper and rope making. However, with the constitution of the HRMS, this lease was given to the society; thus strengthening the villagers' involvement with the protection of hill areas. In the interests of the local labour, the HRMS charged less than half of what the contractor charged for cutting grass and *bhabbar*.

Between 1983 and 1988, the HRMS paid Rs. 5,37,965 to Haryana Forest Department as lease money and earned Rs. 7,94,231 as gross income from sale of fodder grass and *bhabbar*, earning a net profit of Rs. 2,56,266.

The concept of joint forest management was introduced in 1990. As per this, the profit from sale of *bhabbar* was to be shared between the Forest Department and the HRMS in 25:75 ratio. As a result, the society's income from the sale of *bhabbar* declined significantly. There were certain other factors that also contributed to the decline in income from *bhabbar*. The main buyer of this raw material for making paper was the Ballarpur Paper Mills, Yamunanagar. With the society managing the forest, the lease previously available to the mill, at very easy terms was denied. The price of this raw material went up substantially for the mill. Over time, the mill changed its paper-making technology to use eucalyptus instead of *bhabbar* as the raw material. Another factor was the dispute that arose between the neighbouring villages over the sharing of forest resources. The Haryana Forest Department could not help in resolving them to the satisfaction of all the parties.

DEVELOPMENT INDICATORS

With the increase in income, both from farm and dairy sectors, the village economy has made a quantum jump. The villagers began spending part of their income for constructing houses and part of it on acquiring assets and modern gadgets (Table II).

The overall economics of the project, in respect of both farm and dairy sectors, was worked out, taking the initial cost of the project as Rs. 2.0 lacs in 1978. Considering the life of the project as 30 years and a discount rate of 10 per cent, the benefit-cost ratio worked out to be 1.8:1.

TABLE 15.2 Household Assets in Sukhomajri

Items	*Before Project 1975*	*After Project 2000*
A. DOMESTIC		
Bicycle	9	78
Sewing Machine	3	73
Transistor	1	63
Scooter/Motor Cycle	–	42
Television	–	67
Fridge	–	27
Telephone	–	8
L.P. Gas	–	7
Coolers	–	6
B. FARM		
Tractor	–	3
Tubewell	–	4
Thresher	–	5

Source: Central Soil and Water Conservation Training Institute, Research Centre, Chandigarh.

CONCLUSION

A prescriptive approach for organising and operationalising self-help does not work. The wisdom of the locals is essential for the success of any programme concerned with the development of a local area. The advice taken by the Central Soil and Water Conservation Training Institute's officials from the village elders amply illustrates this point. The Ramon Magasaysay Award winner Rajinder Singh asked for advice from the village elders when he began his work in Rajasthan's Alwar District. Singh and two of his companions agreed that they would follow whatever the *samaaj* (community) directed them to do (Kishwar, 2001). Hence, people's needs and problems must be identified and local wisdom tapped at the outset.

Outsiders have worked as critical catalytic agents in the initiation and sustenance of self-help groups. The highly committed officials of the Central

Soil and Water Conservation Research and Training Institute, Research Centre, Chandigarh performed this role at Sukhomajri. The centre developed the technology for earthen dams, using the Ford Foundation grant. Further, regular communication was maintained between the officials of the Centre and the villagers motivating them in their conservation efforts. Humility, open-mindedness and a high spirit of service should be the essential qualities in the persons who work as *catalytic agents*. Hence, officials with a commitment to development can be the ideal catalytic agents for self-help groups.

The shelter of an organisational umbrella is required by self-help groups sooner or later. This gives them an identity on the basis of which they can deal with other agencies. Further, it also satisfies the requirements of aid-giving agencies. The active involvement of the research centre in getting the Ford Foundation grant finances to the Sukhomajri project was crucial. Further, the setting up of the Hill Resources Management Society a few years after the inception of the project to take over its management and deal with the Forest Department and other agencies illustrates this point. We also have the case of Mohammad Yunus, the innovator of the micro-credit system in the villages of Bangladesh. Banks refused to lend money to the poor. Yunus therefore decided to set up the Grameen Bank in 1983, nearly 13 years after the initial step of lending to the poor and initiating them to self-employment measures. The Grameen Bank is now a component of the World Bank having grown into a 1.45 billion pounds sterling business, that lends an average of 21 million pounds sterling a month (Bhanumathy, 1999). It would not be amiss to make a reference here to Tarun Bharat Sangh, (TBS), a defunct NGO that was revived by Shri Rajinder Singh to satisfy the conditions of aid-givers. To start with, TBS got a grant of 40 tonnes of wheat from CASA of UK (a church based international organisation). This became the basis for a locally organised food for work programme to undertake building of check dams, *johads* (ponds) and other water harvesting structures in the area (Kishwar, 2001).

The culture of self-help needs to be consciously propagated. The research centre played an important role in this and the Hill Resources Management Society continued in the same spirit. Similarly, in Gopalpura Water Resource Management Project in Rajasthan, the Tarun Bharat Sangh made an effort to play a role other than that of an efficient substitute for the dysfunctional Public Works Department of the government. It added a message of self-respect to the self-help campaign in motion. They resolved that they would support the building of *johads* only in those villages that voluntarily gave up the making and consumption of alcohol. Far from creating a resentment, it further strengthened the credentials of the organisation (Kishwar, 2001).

The government, instead of providing support, almost treats the self-help groups like adversaries with whom mutually beneficial terms have to be negotiated. The Haryana Forest Department, which did not acknowledge the existence of the Sukhomajri catchment while it was barren, began to evince an interest in the same when it started earning revenue. The plantation of *bhabbar* and other forest produce increased the value of this region and the government stepped in to share the profits. The concept of joint forest management was a unilateral decision of the government and the people had to fall in with its wishes. A similar situation was experienced in Alwar district of Rajasthan when the rejuvenated water bodies resulted in a thriving aquatic life. The villagers had not only prohibited fishing but had devised special rituals to encourage feeding of the fish. The Fisheries Department of the Rajasthan government began to issue fishing contracts to commercial interests from outside the area in order to reap profits.

Discipline through collective resolves is effective. The people of Sukhomajri undertook the protection of forests through the practice of social fencing. They protected the hilly watersheds from overgrazing and illicit cutting of vegetation. This task of preventing the denudation of the hills and catchments was almost impossible for the Forest Department to accomplish.

REFERENCES

1. Arya, Swaran Lata and J.S. Samra, 'Revisiting watershed management institutions in Haryana Shivaliks, India', *Central Soil and Water Conservation Research and Training Institute, Research Centre*, Chandigarh, 2001.
2. Bhanumathy, K.P., 'He brought the micro-credit revolution to B'Desh', *The Tribune*, Nov. 25, 1999.
3. Central Soil and Water Conservation Research and Training Institute, 'The Sukhomajri watershed management project: A success story of participatory approach', CSWCRTI, Research Centre, Chandigarh, 2000.
4. Government of India, Planning Commission, *Approach Paper to Ninth Five Year Plan (1997–2002)*, New Delhi, 1997.
5. Kishwar, Madhu, 'Villages in Rajasthan overcome sarkari dependence—profile of Rajendra Singh and his work', *Manushi*, No. 123, March–April 2001.
6. Mahapatra, Richard, 'Sukhomajri at the crossroads', *Down To Earth*, December 15, 1998.
7. National Bank for Agriculture and Rural Development, 2000, *Self-help Groups: why and how*? Regional Office, Chandigarh.
8. Prasad, Kamta (Ed.), *NGOs and Socio-Economic Development Opportunities*, Deep and Deep Publications Pvt. Ltd., New Delhi, 2000.

Index

Accountable and citizen friendly, 3, 24
Administrative reforms, 3, 4, 24, 52
Administrative Reforms Commission, 48
Aristotle, 16
Autonomous District Councils, 128, 131–133

Bhoomi and Nondani, 100
Bhuria committee, 134
Bureau of Police Research and Development, 48
Bureaucracy, 1, 39–45
  organisation, 41
  policy makers, 40
  society, 42

Central Soil and Water Conservation Research and Training Institute, 137
Citizen centric, 62, 63
City civic centre, 77
Commission on Global Governance, 18
Community based organisations, 23, 24
Community Internet Centres, 124
Computer Assisted Registration, 99
Confederation of Indian Industry, 36, 37
Controller of Certifying Authorities, 64, 66
Criminal justice system, 47, 50
Criminal trials, 49
Cybernetic state, 39

Decentralized governance, 7–9, 23
Deconcentration, 7
Democratic decentralization, 13, 128
Denhardt, 41, 42, 43
Department of Administrative Reforms and Public Grievances, 3
Devolution, 7, 8
Digital certification, 63
Digital divide, 59
Digital governance, 87
Direct Reception System, 112, 113
Directive Principles of State Policy, 129
Disaster management, 119, 120

Economy, 33–35
E-governance, 5–27, 32
  applications, 64–68, 100, 122–126
  models, 54
E-government, 54
Esselbrugge, Monique,

Freedom of information, 3
FRIENDS, 6, 102
Front-end computerization, 102, 104–106

GIS, 117–118
Governance, 20–21
  civil, 20–21
  economics, 20
  good governance, 1
  issues and strategies, 9–14, 29–37, 97–99
  political, 20
Governance portal, 63
Gramsat Pilot Project, 112–120
Gyandoot programme, 65

Habitat II, 18–19
Hans, Eric, 39–40

Heeks, Richard, 5, 86, 87
Hill Resources Management Society, 139
Human Development Report, 19–20, 25
Hye, Hasnat Abdul, 21

IGNOU, 31
Information Technology Mission Group, 103
Information and Communication Technology, 5, 70
Information Technology, 52–54, 121–122
  Act, 2000, 25
Information system, 58–60
  environment, 60
  information, 58
  people, 60
  processes, 60
  technology, 59
Institute of Criminology and Forensic Science, 48
Interactive policy making, 9

Jail reforms, 50
Judicial Courts, 49

Kautilya, 16–17
Khajane, 100
Kothari R., 44
Krishi Vigyan Kendra, 110

Law, 47–48
  enforcement, 48
  making, 47
Law Commission, 47, 49
Local self government, 8

Massachusetts Institute of Technology, 37
Ministry of Human Resource Development, 30–31
Ministry of Personnel, Public Grievances, and Pensions, 3, 6
MIS, 118–119
Monopolies and Restrictive Trade Practices Act, 23
Mukhya Vahini, 100

National Informatics Centre, 123
National Police Commission, 46, 48
New economic policy, 1991, 22, 23
New public service, 41

Online services, 71–74, 77–80
Operation knowledge, 30
Organisation for Economic Cooperation and Development, 18

Panchayati Raj, 129
Panchayats, 8
Pierre, J., 40, 45
Privatisation, 8
Public-Private partnership, 80, 98, 107
Public Service Delivery, 1, 2

Responsive service, 2
Russell, Thomas, 31

Saukaryam project, 73
Scheduled areas, 134
Self-help group, 136
Seventy third and seventy fourth constitutional amendment 1992, 8, 128, 130
Social fencing, 138
Social security, 64
State Security Commission, 48
Statutory Criminal Justice Commission, 49
Sukhomajri, 136, 137
  watershed management project, 136
Sustainable human development, 21, 22
Svara, James H., 40

Tarun Bharat Sangh, 141
Transparency, 35, 36

UGC, 30

UNDP, 19
UNESCO, 19, 31
United Nations Language Networking Scheme, 37
User association, 111, 117

Village Councils, 128, 132, 133
  Act, 131
Virtual community, 56
Visakhapatnam Municipal Corporation, 73

Willy McCourt, 1
World Bank, 17
World Development Report, 29
World Wide Web, 76